Ivy Global

New PSAT 3 Practice Tests
Edition 1.1

Resources & Downloads:

IVYGLOBAL.COM/STUDY

PASSWORD: greenbook

NEW PSAT 3 PRACTICE TESTS

This publication was written and edited by the team at Ivy Global.

Editor-in-Chief: Sarah Pike
Producers: Lloyd Min and Junho Suh

Editors: Sacha Azor, Corwin Henville, Nathan Létourneau, and Kristin Rose

Contributors: Natalia Cole, Laurel Durning-Hammond, Elizabeth Hilts, Somin Lee, James Levine, Mark Mendola, and Gideon Ng

Proofreaders: Ali Candib, Shavumiyaa Chandrabalan, Lisa Faieta, Lei Huang, James Levine, Yolanda Song, and Adam Wolsky

This product was developed by Ivy Global, a pioneering education company that delivers a wide range of educational services.

E-mail: publishing@ivyglobal.com
Website: http://www.ivyglobal.com

Contents

Chapter 1
Introduction

Section 1
About this Book

Welcome, students and parents! The New PSAT 3 Practice Tests were created to help you prepare for the newly redesigned PSAT. In this book you will find information and strategies for approaching all sections of the test: Reading, Writing, and Math. You can apply what you've learned by practicing with the three full-length diagnostic tests.

If you would like more in-depth review of the concepts tested by the PSAT, you can also check out Ivy Global's New SAT Guide. It contains hundreds of pages of lessons, strategies, and practice, nearly all of which applies to the PSAT. You can read more in the Using the New SAT Guide section of this book. For more information or to purchase our new SAT and PSAT publications, please visit us at sat.ivyglobal.com.

Also be sure to check out ivyglobal.com/study for bonuses related to this book. As an owner of the New PSAT 3 Practice Tests, you can access additional resources to support your studying, such as extra scoring sheets and answer explanations.

If you have any questions or feedback, we would love to hear from you. Send us an email anytime at publishing@ivyglobal.com.

We hope you enjoy this book, and wish you the best of luck with your academic goals!

Section 2
About the PSAT

What is the PSAT?

The PSAT is a standardized test written and administered by the College Board, and cosponsored by the National Merit Scholarship Corporation. It is designed to assess students' skills in critical reading, mathematics, and writing.

Beginning in the fall of 2015, there will be three PSAT tests: the PSAT 8/9, the PSAT 10, and the PSAT/NMSQT (PSAT/National Merit Scholarship Qualifying Test). Students can take these tests in eighth or ninth grade, tenth grade, and tenth or eleventh grade, respectively. This book is particularly geared towards preparation for the PSAT/NMSQT, and when we say "PSAT" that's the test we mean. However, the advice we give applies to all three tests.

Unlike SAT scores, PSAT scores are not reported to colleges. They are, however, still an important part of the road to college. The PSAT evaluates the same skills as the SAT, using the same format, with scores reported to students on a similar scale. That means that your performance on the PSAT can give you valuable feedback about how ready you are for the SAT.

It can also tell you if there are particular areas you should focus on as you prepare to take the SAT. If you ace the reading section but don't perform as well in math, for example, you can tailor your SAT studying to mastering math concepts, while taking it easier on your reading practice.

When you take the PSAT/NMSQT you can also sign up for the College Board's Student Search Service, which is a free way to receive information from colleges and scholarship programs looking for students like you. Eleventh graders may also qualify to be considered for National Merit Scholarships and other scholarship and recognition programs if they score well on the PSAT/NMSQT.

TAKING THE TEST

Unlike the SAT, which is offered year-round, the PSAT is only offered on two test dates in the same month. The PSAT 8/9 and the PSAT/NMSQT are administered in the fall; the PSAT 10 is administered in the spring.

Usually, students take the PSAT when it is administered at their schools without needing to sign up individually. Families should ask students' advisors or guidance counselors whether their schools will be administering the PSAT and if so, when. If your school is not offering the PSAT, you cannot make the test date your school selected, or you are home-schooled, you can still take the test. You will need to find a school near you that is administering the PSAT and contact them to request that they let you take it there. You should do so at least four months before the test date. For more information and to search for local schools administering the PSAT, go to the College Board's website at www.collegeboard.org.

Students can take the PSAT/NMSQT twice: once in tenth grade, and once in eleventh grade. Only eleventh graders can be considered for National Merit Scholarship opportunities; however, tenth graders can benefit from early feedback on their strengths and weaknesses.

If you need accommodations for a documented disability to take the PSAT, you must request them at least seven weeks in advance. The specific deadline for submitting relevant materials varies from year to year, so to be safe you should begin the request process in the spring before the fall of the test, or at the beginning of the fall semester for the PSAT 10.

WHAT'S NEW?

The College Board is implementing significant changes to the SAT that will take effect in the spring of 2016. Because the PSAT tests the same material in the same format as the SAT, the PSAT will also be undergoing significant changes. The new PSAT will actually be administered before the new SAT, in the fall of 2015, since the PSAT is meant to be taken before the SAT.

The most important changes to the test are in the content covered. The Reading Test will be shifting exclusively to passage-based questions, which refer to a passage and assess your comprehension of the passage and command of textual evidence. This means there are no more sentence completion questions. The new Writing Test will also use only passage-based questions, where you'll read a passage that includes some errors, and determine how to correct or improve sentences, paragraphs, or the passage as a whole. In both tests, you'll see a wider variety of passage types than on the old PSAT.

The Math Test will focus on the core math areas of algebra and data analysis, and will also feature more questions relevant to real-life situations. Overall, it will be more closely linked to what you're learning in school, instead of featuring lots of tricky "brainteaser" problems like the old test did.

Like the new SAT, the new PSAT will also eliminate the guessing penalty of ¼ of a point for every wrong answer, and it will reduce answer choices from 5 (A to E) to 4 (A to D). This means you have a better chance of guessing the right answer and nothing to lose by trying!

As we mentioned earlier, there are now three levels of the PSAT instead of just one. All three of them will use the same basic format, though the PSAT 8/9 will be scored slightly differently from the PSAT 10 and PSAT/NMSQT. The differences are because the exams are written for students in different grades.

THE REDESIGNED TEST

The new PSAT is 2 hours and 45 minutes long. That time breaks down like this:

- 95-minute Evidence-Based Reading and Writing Test
    - Reading Test (60 minutes, 47 questions)
    - Writing and Language Test (35 minutes, 44 questions)

- 70-minute Math Test
    - No-calculator allowed section (25 minutes, 17 questions)
    - Calculator allowed section (45 minutes, 31 questions)

There is no Essay on the PSAT.

The Reading Test, Writing Test, and the two combined sections of the Math Test will each receive a test score on a scale from 8-38. These test scores will also be converted into section scores. The Reading Test and Writing Test will be scored together as Evidence-Based Reading and Writing on a scale from 160-760; the Math Test by itself will also be scored on a scale from 160-760. Those two section scores will be added together for a total composite score from 320-1520.

In addition, the new PSAT will feature a set of subscores, which focus on certain types of content in either the Reading, Writing, or Math Test. Each subscore will be reported on a scale of 1-15. There will be seven subscores reported in total: Heart of Algebra, Problem Solving and Data Analysis, Passport to Advanced Math, Expression of Ideas, Standard English Conventions, Words in Context, and Command of Evidence. Each score will be based on a range of 14 to 24 questions that test particular skillsets.

The new PSAT will also include cross-test scores, which measure analytical thinking in a particular subject area. Each cross-test score will be reported on a scale of 8-38. There will be two cross-test scores reported: Analysis in History/Social Studies and Analysis in Science. Each score will be based on a selection of relevant questions throughout all sections of the test.

Later in this chapter, we'll go over what the different sections of the test look like in more detail. We'll also go over some general test-taking tips, and explain how to use Ivy Global's New SAT Guide to study for the PSAT.

Section 3
Approaching the PSAT

In this section, we'll go over general strategies you can use to prepare for the PSAT using this book and Ivy Global's New SAT Guide. Later, we'll talk about tips for test day and discuss the individual test sections in more detail.

Know the Test

The first thing to understand about the PSAT is the style and structure of the test itself. The PSAT is a standardized test, which means that although the specific questions will change from year to year, the format is always the same. Knowing the format in advance will save you valuable time on test day, as you'll already be familiar with the instructions and the type of thinking you'll be asked to do. You can find the general format of the test in the previous section, and more specific information about each part of the test in their respective sections.

A standardized test is not like the tests your English or Math teacher creates for your class, although you may have taken standardized tests in school before. The PSAT is scored not by a human, but by a computer that "reads" your answer sheet. This means that filling in your answer bubbles neatly and completely is essential, since a computer can't tell that you got the right answer but didn't fill the bubble in completely. Bubbling correctly is a habit you can practice with the tests in this book.

It also means there's no partial credit for knowing how to solve a problem but making a computation error. Checking your work is always a good idea, but it's especially important on a standardized test. Budget your time to leave a few minutes at the end to double-check your answers so you don't miss a question you understood but entered incorrectly into your calculator.

It also helps to know in advance that each question on the PSAT is worth one point regardless of how hard or easy it is. The new PSAT also has no penalty for wrong answers, so you should always guess without worrying that you might hurt your score. Later we'll talk more about how to make the best use of these facts, but knowing them is a good start.

STUDY TIPS

When you study for the PSAT, make your space as calm and free of distractions as possible. Leave your phone and other electronics out of reach, so you won't be tempted to look at them. If you're timing yourself on a practice test, set a loud alarm instead of looking at your phone or computer screen.

Don't try to do too much at once. It's hard to learn much by the end of a four-hour study session, especially if your brain is already tired from a day at school. It's also difficult to master several new concepts at once. Set aside moderate amounts of time during which you plan to focus on one or two concepts, and then build in a review day every other week.

Never stay up late studying. In addition to making you feel tired in the morning, losing sleep can harm your health over the long run. Sleep is also when your brain solidifies new information, so it's a crucial part of the learning process.

Section 4
Using the New SAT Guide

The New SAT Guide is designed to be used to study for the SAT. However, it can also be used to study for the PSAT/NMSQT, because the two exams test the same concepts at similar levels of difficulty. How you use it will depend on your approach to studying. There are two basic approaches to studying for the PSAT: general preparation and targeted practice.

General Preparation
PART 1

The New SAT Guide is structured to help you build your general test-taking skills. However, that doesn't mean you should just work through it cover-to-cover—that would leave all your math preparation till the end, while letting your reading practice fade from memory by test day.

However, the information and exercises within each chapter are arranged from more basic to more advanced. This means that it's a good idea to work through the content within chapters in order, while alternating which chapter you work on.

For example, you might set yourself a Monday, Wednesday, and Friday study schedule. For your first week, you might work through the first part of Approaching the Reading Test (p. 34-46) on Monday, the first part of Approaching the Writing Test (p. 263-268) on Wednesday, and the first part of Approaching the Math Test (p. 456-460) on Friday. There's no Essay on the PSAT, so you can save that chapter for when you're focusing exclusively on the SAT.

Here's a sample study schedule that will get you through the essentials for each subject. Work through the practice sets at the end of individual parts to make sure you've understood the concepts you're practicing.

	Monday	Wednesday	Friday
Week 1	Approaching the Reading Test, p. 34-46	Approaching the Writing Test, p. 263-268	Approaching the Math Test, p. 456-464
Week 2	Reading Test Questions, p. 47-70	Writing Test Questions, p. 269-282	Problem Solving, p. 465-481
Week 3	Information and Ideas Questions I, p. 108-130	Grammar Review, p. 283-302	Heart of Algebra I, p. 509-536
Week 4	Information and Ideas Questions II, p. 131-150	Common Grammar Errors, p. 303-314	Heart of Algebra II, p. 537-576
Week 5	Rhetoric Questions, p. 152-188	Development of Ideas, p. 336-342	Passport to Advanced Math basics, p. 588-620
Week 6	Synthesis Questions, p. 190-216	Effective Language Use, p. 359-372	Problem Solving and Data Analysis basics, p. 648-680

Depending on your schedule, you can also split up these sessions into smaller segments by stopping when you hit a practice set. Alternately, you can add in some of the sections listed below in Targeted Practice that have been left out of this roadmap to the basics.

Make sure you plan ahead so you leave yourself enough time to finish all your preparation before your test date.

TARGETED PRACTICE
PART 2

If you feel confident that you are stronger in some areas than others, you may choose to use your time to target mostly the skills you are weaker in, especially if your PSAT test date is fast-approaching. For example, if you know for sure you have mastered some math concepts but not others, you may choose not to review the math concepts you already know. That means if you know you're rock-solid on Absolute Value (p. 531-536), you can choose to skip ahead to Systems of Equations and Inequalities (p. 537-544).

If you are not sure what your strengths and weaknesses are, you can start by taking one of the tests in this book to see how you score in each section. The questions in the Reading and Writing Tests in particular may look different from what you've encountered in English class in school. That is why becoming familiar with PSAT questions is so helpful, even if you are a strong student.

Either way, you can pick and choose what you want to study from the New SAT Guide. The following tables, broken down by subject, will point you to whatever you might wish to focus on. Do note that although the overall format of the PSAT is the same as that of the SAT, there are a few differences in terms of how many questions of each type there are per section and overall.

READING TEST TOPICS

Topic	Pages in the New SAT Guide *First Edition*
Active Reading	p. 34-46
Reading Test Questions	p. 47-52
Choosing Answers	p. 53-70
Literature Passages	p. 73-80
Science Passages	p. 81-88
Social Science and Historical Passages	p. 89-94
Passages with Graphics	p. 95-100

Paired Passages	p. 101-106
Words and Phrases in Context	p. 109-114
Explicit and Implicit Meaning	p. 115-122
Central Ideas and Relationships	p. 123-130
Evidence in a Passage	p. 131-136
Analogical Reasoning	p. 137-142
Analyzing Word Choice	p. 153-158
Analyzing Text Structure	p. 159-164
Point of View and Purpose	p. 165-170
Analyzing Arguments	p. 171-180
Paired Passage Questions	p. 191-198
Passages with Graphs Question	p. 199-206

WRITING TEST TOPICS

Topic	Pages in the New SAT Guide *First Edition*
Reading the Passages	p. 263-268
Reading the Questions	p. 269-274
Answering the Questions	p. 275-282
Parts of Speech	p. 284-288
Sentences	p. 289-302
Common Grammar Errors	p. 303-314
Harder Grammar Errors	p. 315-324
Development of Ideas	p. 336-342
Graphics	p. 343-352
Organizing Ideas	p. 353-358
Effective Language Use	p. 359-366

MATH TEST TOPICS

Topic	Pages in the New SAT Guide *First Edition*
Problem Solving Strategies	p. 465-481
Integers	p. 483-485
Operations	p. 486-487

Fractions	p. 488-493
Ratios, Percentages, Proportions, and Rates	p. 494-497
Exponents and Radicals	p. 498-499
Scientific Notation	p. 500-502
Algebraic Expressions	p. 509-514
Linear Equations	p. 515-522
Inequalities	p. 523-530
Absolute Value	p. 531-536
Systems of Equations and Inequalities	p. 537-544
Linear Functions	p. 545-550
Interpreting Equations	p. 551-556
Graphing Equations	p. 557-576
Polynomial Expressions	p. 588-594
Factoring Polynomials	p. 595-602
Quadratic Equations	p. 603-610
Quadratic Functions	p. 611-620
Advanced Equations	p. 621-628
Applications of Functions	p. 629-636
Measurement and Units	p. 648-656
Properties of Data	p. 657-672
Ratios, Percentages, Proportions, and Rates (Advanced)	p. 673-680
Probability and Statistics	p. 681-700
Modeling Data	p. 701-710
Using Data as Evidence	p. 711-734
Introductory Geometry	p. 736-756
Right Triangles	p. 757-768
Radians and the Unit Circle	p. 769-780
Circles	p. 781-790
Complex Numbers	p. 791-796

*If you have a newer edition of the New SAT Guide, please check online at ivyglobal.com/study for updated page numbers.

EXTRA PRACTICE
PART 3

The tests in this book are designed to provide realistic examples of PSAT questions, so you should take advantage of that! Make time to work through all of them, as practice is the most effective form of preparation.

Strive for a realistic testing environment by removing distractions, and time yourself so you get a sense of whether you're achieving the pace you need. However, if you do run out of time, don't just stop like you would on the real test. Mark where you were in the test when your alarm rang, and finish the rest of the section. Alternately, you can come back and try the remaining questions at a later time. That way, you still make full use of the test. You can read more about managing your time on the PSAT in the next section.

If you don't have three straight hours to take a practice test, it's okay to split the test up into sections. You can do the Reading Test one night, the Writing Test the next, and the two parts of the Math Test the third. However, be sure to practice at least once with a full-length test before your real PSAT test date.

The sections in the New SAT Guide have comprehensive practice sets designed to help you practice a specific number of techniques at a time. You can set aside separate times to do those as a form of review, if you do not complete them as you work through each section. There are also full-length practice sections at the end of each chapter that add up to an additional SAT practice test; although you're studying for the PSAT, taking these can give you additional practice on the topics the test will cover.

When you go over your answers, don't stop at marking how many you got right or wrong. Check your wrong answers and see if you can understand why they're wrong. If you can't figure out why the right answer is correct, go back and reread the relevant sections of the New SAT Guide that cover what the question is testing. This will both reinforce what you've learned and help you stay alert for potential errors on the day of the test.

Answer explanations are available at:
ivyglobal.com/study

TEST DAY

PART 4

On the day of the PSAT, you want to maximize your chances of success. Here are some general tips to make sure you can do your best.

BEFORE THE TEST

On the night before your test, study only lightly, if at all. You won't be able to fully learn anything new at this point. Review up to three tricky areas if you want, but the most important thing you can do the night before the PSAT—or any big test—is give yourself a solid night of sleep.

Lay out your clothes for the next day so that getting dressed goes smoothly. It's a good idea to wear layers so you can adjust to the room's temperature. Also lay out the bag you'll take, making sure to bring:

- At least two sharpened No. 2 pencils with erasers
- A calculator with new batteries and back-up batteries
- A non-beeping watch
- Snack and water bottle
- Photo ID (only if you're testing at a school you do not attend)

If you're taking the PSAT at a school that's not your own, make sure you or whoever's taking you knows how to get there. In the morning, make sure you eat a healthy breakfast—you don't want to be stuck past the two-hour mark with an empty stomach!

MANAGING YOUR TIME

The PSAT is 2 hours and 45 minutes long, with 139 questions total. Remember that time between sections isn't transferable; you're given a set amount of time for each section and you can't proceed to the next section if you finish early. When you take the practice tests in this book, be sure to time yourself so you can get a sense for how long each section takes to complete. This will come in handy on the real test, when you can gauge whether you are on track to finish on time or whether you need to speed up.

It's important not to get too stuck on any single question and to move through the test at a steady pace. Don't waste 10 minutes on a question that stumps you, only to find that you don't have enough time to answer the things you know inside out. Each question is worth just one point, no matter how hard it is. If you're stuck on a problem, make your best guess and move on. Circle the problem in your question booklet so you can go back to it if you have time at the end to check your answers. Remember not to make any stray marks on your answer sheet, even when you guess.

Educated Guessing

Time management is key because you want to be able to answer as many questions as possible, especially since the College Board has eliminated the guessing penalty for the new PSAT. You should try to answer every single question because you have nothing to lose— just more points to gain! At the same time, you should aim for a balance between quality and quantity. Budget your time so you can get to every question while still reading each question and answer choice carefully.

If, after reading the question and each answer choice closely, you are still unsure of the answer, you should guess. There might be times when you really just don't understand a question at all. For those situations, it's best to pick out a letter in advance that you will use to guess. Using just one letter makes it easier to guess than picking a different letter each time.

However, even on questions you're not sure about, your guesses don't always have to be random. You can up your chances of getting the right answer using the Process of Elimination.

As you read through the answer choices, don't select an answer on your first read-through. For each option, choose to either "knock it out" if you know it is incorrect, or leave it open to reconsider later if it seems possible. Once you have assessed all of the answer choices, you can compare any that you left open and select the best one. Even if you've only managed to eliminate one, that takes your chances of guessing correctly from 25% to 33%. If you can eliminate two choices, you have a 50-50 chance of getting the answer right!

Section 5
Introduction to the Reading Test

In this section, we'll go over the format of the Reading Test so you know exactly what to expect on test day. Then we'll talk about strategies for approaching the various passage types, as well as different kinds of questions you can expect to see. Finally, we'll go over some tips for building good reading habits that will help you on the PSAT and beyond.

APPROACHING THE READING TEST
PART 1

THE STRUCTURE OF THE TEST

The PSAT/NMSQT Reading Test contains four individual passages and one set of paired passages. Each passage—or, in the case of the paired passages, the combined set—is between 500 and 750 words long, and is accompanied by a set of 9 or 10 questions. The Reading Test will always include a total of 3,000 words in the passages and 47 questions. Two passages will always have accompanying graphics you'll be asked questions about.

All passages in the Reading Test come from previously published sources, and may represent a variety of tones and styles. The chart below shows the specific breakdown of passage types that you will see on the Reading Test. These passage types will be discussed in detail in the next part.

Passage Type	Topics	Number of Passages
Literature	Classic and contemporary literature from the United States and around the world	1
Science	Both basic concepts and recent developments in the natural sciences, including Earth science, biology, chemistry, and physics	2
History/Social Studies	Anthropology, communication studies, economics, education, human geography, law, linguistics, political science, psychology, and sociology	1
Founding Documents or Great Global Conversation	Historically important, foundational texts from the United States (Founding Documents), other historically and culturally important works dealing with issues at the heart of civic and political life (Great Global Conversation)	1

ACTIVE READING

You always want to make an effort to understand the content of a passage while you're reading it, rather than trying to make sense of it only once you reach the questions. That way, you'll save time and ensure that you have the necessary context to answer all questions.

This means you need to be an active reader, interacting with the passages to keep track of the information you'll be tested on.

One strategy for active reading is to use your pencil to mark up the passage as you read. You can underline significant concepts and add your own notes and symbols to highlight what's most important. Don't go overboard, or your notes will be too crowded to be useful. Instead, seek to identify one to three main ideas in each paragraph. A good rule of thumb for identifying main ideas is to look for information that answers the *5 w*'s: who, what, where, when, and why.

1. **Who** is involved in this passage? In non-fiction, look for the people being discussed—artists, scholars, scientists, politicians—as well as the person writing, especially in Founding Documents or Great Global Conversation passages. In literature, look for the characters, including the narrator if the passage is written in the first-person point of view.
2. **What** is being discussed? Is the passage about specific events, theories, or ideas? Look for the major concepts in each section of the passage.
3. **Where** are the events taking place? This can mean a specific location (a science laboratory) or a general setting (the United States).
4. **When** are the events in the passage taking place? It's usually more important to know the order in which things occur than to know specific dates. For Founding Documents and Great Global Conversation documents especially, the "when" also includes the events the passage is in response to or trying to influence.
5. **Why** is the information in this passage important? How are the ideas in the passage connected, and what is the author's purpose for writing the passage?

You can also use the space next to the text to jot down quick summaries of the main point of each paragraph. Summarizing helps ensure that you understood what you read, and it helps you avoid drifting off and reading words without any comprehension. Making a three-to-six-word summary of each paragraph—think newspaper headlines—can cement your understanding and make it easier to find evidence later when you're answering questions.

These tips can be used for all passages you will encounter on the Reading Test, but it's also important to be aware of how you will need to adapt your approach for different passage types.

PASSAGE TYPES
PART 2

LITERATURE PASSAGES

There is one Literature passage in the Reading section of the PSAT. Usually it is an excerpt from a novel or short story, which may be recently published or older. These older passages might contain unfamiliar words or phrases, but most of the language will be understandable to modern readers. Literature passages will never use graphics or be presented as paired passages.

Literature passages generally tell a story or describe a scene, object, or character, and unlike most other passages on the PSAT, they typically have underlying meanings that may not be stated directly. Your goals for a Literature passage are to follow what is actually being described, to look for potential additional meanings, and to pay attention to the author's use of language and literary techniques to convey both explicit and implicit meanings.

Literature passages might contain figurative language, or language used in a creative or unusual way. The PSAT might ask you to interpret specific pieces of figurative language, or to analyze their effects or the author's reasons for including them.

The PSAT might also ask you about the author's characterization—how the author conveys information about the people in the passage. This might be plainly stated, but it might also be expressed through details about the character's actions, appearance, or feelings. As with figurative language, the surface meaning—what's immediately apparent—might not be the most important thing about a particular character detail.

SCIENCE PASSAGES

The PSAT has two science passages, usually taken from magazines, newspapers, or non-fiction books on popular science. The passages will be about the natural or physical sciences—physics, biology, astronomy, chemistry, or similar fields. They will always be from contemporary sources, reflecting recent scientific endeavors and discoveries.

On the science passages, you won't be tested on your own scientific knowledge; the PSAT will never ask about scientific facts that are not discussed in the passage. Instead, the PSAT is assessing your skill in comprehending ideas presented in scientific language.

Science passages might be one of two types: explanatory or argumentative. Explanatory passages provide information about a topic. Their purpose is simply to inform the reader of a discovery, set of facts, or conversation in the scientific community. In an explanatory passage, it's important to understand the facts presented and how they relate to each other. In some cases, such as articles about recent experiments, it might also be important to understand the methods through which people came to know those facts.

Argumentative passages, by contrast, take a certain position on the issue they're discussing, and provide evidence to support their position. Often they're sharing an opinion not only about an interpretation of the available evidence, but about what people should do with that information. In these passages, it's especially important to look out for how authors construct their arguments logically, as well as what language they use to make their arguments persuasive to readers.

HISTORY/SOCIAL STUDIES PASSAGES

One of the History/Social Studies passages you encounter will be very similar to the Science passages: drawn from a contemporary source and describing a current issue or discovery. The difference is that the History/Social Studies passage will relate to a field in the social sciences—economics, linguistics, sociology, and so on—so it will deal primarily with human beings. However, your general approach to these passages can be largely the same as your approach to Science passages.

The other History/Social Studies passage will be very different. This one will be drawn from either the Founding Documents of the United States—documents such as the Declaration of Independence, the Federalist papers, or the U.S. Constitution—or the Great Global Conversation, the ongoing worldwide discourse about civic life carried on in speeches and written works by politicians, activists, and other leaders.

These historical documents address complex and potentially abstract topics such as the nature of liberty, the role of government, or the arguments for or against war. Like Literature passages, historical passages will often involve careful use of language designed for a particular emotional or rhetorical effect, and the PSAT might ask you to evaluate the impact of a word or phrase, as well as the author's purpose in using it.

It's important to pay attention to the main point of the passage, which is often an argument the speaker or author is making. In historical documents, it can be tricky to hone in on the main point because the language is often more complicated than what you might be used to reading. This is where sharp, concise paragraph summaries can come in handy: by highlighting the most important part of each paragraph, you can get a sense of what the passage as a whole is saying, without getting distracted or confused by the details.

PAIRED PASSAGES

One of the five sets of questions on the Reading section—either History/Social Studies or Science—will be about a set of two shorter passages, rather than one longer one. These two passages are always about the same general subject, but they approach it from different angles.

This can take many forms. The two passages might present the arguments for and against something, or one might be a straightforward explanatory passage while the other makes an argument for a specific position. The second passage might be a closer look at something the first passage describes in broader terms. While they'll share an overall topic, they may differ in purpose, focus, claims, interpretations, or style.

You can approach paired passages the way you approach History/Social Studies and Science passages, but also keep an eye out for significant distinctions between the passages. While reading the second passage, for example, you might want to circle or underline statements that contradict or support claims made in the first passage.

PASSAGES WITH GRAPHICS

One History/Social Studies and one Science passage will contain graphic elements, either one or two for each passage. These might be graphs, charts, or diagrams that display data or concepts discussed in or relevant to the topic of the passage. You will be asked questions about the graphic or its relationship to the text.

Read the passage first to gain context for what the graphic is showing. Don't spend a lot of time trying to interpret the graphic fully. Instead, look for the title and any relevant labels, which will tell you what it's demonstrating. If it's a graph, make sure you know what each axis represents and what units the graph is using. Take a moment to familiarize yourself with the layout, because that will enable you to quickly find whatever information the related questions ask about.

READING TEST QUESTIONS
PART 3

Now that we've gone over different types and aspects of passages in the Reading Test, let's take a look at what kinds of questions you'll be facing. These fall into three broad categories: Information and Ideas, Rhetoric, and Synthesis.

INFORMATION AND IDEAS

One of the major skills assessed on the Reading Test is your skill in interpreting Information and Ideas. Information and Ideas questions ask about the content of the passage you've read. Sometimes these will be very straightforward, asking you for the explicit meaning or best available summary for the passage or a specific section of the passage.

Other questions will require more analysis. Information and Ideas questions might ask you to assess the implicit meaning—something that is strongly suggested but not directly stated—of a particular piece of the text. They also might ask you to identify the central ideas or themes of the text; your notes can be useful here. You may also be asked to analyze relationships between events, concepts, or people.

Information and Ideas questions might also ask you to think beyond the passage by making connections from an aspect of the text to something else. This might involve extrapolating information from the text and applying it to a different context. It might also involve identifying which of four situations is the most analogous to one described in the text.

One useful strategy for Information and Ideas questions is the Process of Elimination. You can often rule out some incorrect answers by eliminating any answer choices that contradict something stated in the passage. You can also knock out options that may be true generally but are not addressed in the passage. Also watch for summaries that are overly specific, honing in on something that was really only a supporting detail rather than a main point.

Information and Ideas questions focus primarily on the content of a passage, but examining the wording of a passage can sometimes help you answer them. Sometimes, information is conveyed through the author's word choices and tone. Transition words and phrases, like "because," "therefore," "in spite of," or "however," give you clues about the chain of cause and effect. Being aware of these kinds of relationships will help you find the best analogy for them, too: look for the analogy with the same relationship between the things described.

Tone is also relevant to questions about what the passage implies or suggests. If a passage takes a harsh, critical tone towards a new invention, for example, you can eliminate any answer choices that state that the passage most strongly suggests something positive about the invention.

RHETORIC

Another skill the PSAT will be assessing on the Reading Test is your command of rhetoric. Rhetoric is persuasive language, and rhetorical analysis involves examining the word choice, structure, and other aspects of a text to understand how an author created a particular effect. Rhetoric questions will ask you to do just that: assess the main effect a word or turn of phrase has in the context of the passage.

Rhetoric questions can also look at broader aspects of the passage. They may ask you to examine the structure of the passage as a whole, or identify the main purpose of the passage or of a particular part of it. They may ask you to identify the point of view or perspective the author of a passage takes, and to think about how that impacts the choices the author made. You may also be asked questions about how an author constructs his or her argument.

Gauging an author's tone will help you answer Rhetoric questions. If an author mostly uses words with positive connotations—words that might not mean "happy" or "good" but which bring up associations with happy or good things—that tells you the author has a positive point of view towards the topic. That means you can eliminate answer choices that state that the author has a negative attitude.

Authors might also use tone to convey differences between certain things in the passage. If the words used to describe one thing have positive connotations, and the words used to describe another thing have negative connotations, that tells you something about how the author views those two things, and potentially about the relationship the passage is trying to establish between them.

Rhetoric questions are especially common in Literature and Great Global Conversation/Founding Documents passages, because the authors of those texts are usually as interested in creating an emotional impact as they are in conveying information. When reading these passages, pay attention to how the author wants the audience to feel as well as what the author wants the audience to know.

SYNTHESIS

The last broad skill the Reading Test will be assessing is Synthesis. Synthesis essentially means "combination," and Synthesis questions will ask you to examine two things at once—either both passages in a paired passage set together, or a passage and its accompanying graphic. These questions will generally come at the end of the question set.

Synthesis questions for paired passages might ask you to identify commonalities or differences between the two passages. These commonalities or differences might be in content, or they might be in tone or point of view. You might also be asked to characterize the relationship between two passages, or to assess whether something in one passage supports an assertion in the other passage.

For all of these types of questions, it will help to look at the notes you've made. If you've already marked places where the two passages overlap or diverge, those notes will serve as a quick reference for potential answers. They can also help you eliminate answers that contradict what you've already noticed.

Synthesis questions for graphics will ask you to interpret the data presented in the graphic, and may also ask you to relate the information from the graphic to the information from the passage. They might also ask you to use information from both the graphic and the passage to extrapolate beyond what's directly stated. Your best bet is to familiarize yourself quickly with how the graphic is set up and what it's presenting, and then look for the specific information the question is asking about.

Synthesis questions on the Reading Test will not ask you to make mathematical calculations.

QUESTION TYPE: WORDS IN CONTEXT

Each passage on the Reading section will have two Words in Context questions. These Words in Context questions might fall under Information and Ideas, or they might fall under Rhetoric.

Words in Context questions under Information and Ideas ask you to determine the meaning of a word as it's being used in a particular sentence. Many words have several subtly different possible meanings, and the answer choices for these questions will always all be potential synonyms for the original word. To find the right answer, try plugging each option into the original sentence and pick the one that doesn't change the meaning of the sentence.

Words in Context questions under Rhetoric ask you to assess the effect of a particular word or phrase in the context of the passage. This could include asking what idea the use of a word or phrase is meant to convey, or having you identify the emotional or persuasive impact of a rhetorical maneuver. Even though these questions are asking about a specific sentence, it's important to keep the whole passage in mind, since you don't want to pick an answer choice that contradicts the passage overall even if, out of context, it might be a plausible reading of the sentence.

QUESTION TYPE: CITING TEXTUAL EVIDENCE

Each passage on the Reading section will have at least two Citing Textual Evidence questions. These are Information and Ideas questions that ask you to pick which lines from the passage provide the best evidence for the answer to the previous question. To answer these, reread the lines you're given and think about how they relate to the assertion you made in answering the previous question.

Remember to think about the main point of the question, and don't get distracted just because an answer choice mentions the same detail that was mentioned in the previous question. That might be the right answer—but the right answer might also be one that doesn't mention that detail at all, instead summarizing the argument that the author was using the detail to support.

CULTIVATING GOOD READING SKILLS
PART 4

Good readers are those who read a lot and read actively. This doesn't mean you have to annotate your favorite book the way you would a passage on the PSAT; it just means that when you read, instead of passively absorbing the text, you try to engage with it. This can mean making sure you understand what's going on, taking note of questions you have, or drawing connections to your life or other things you've read.

Reading with the sole goal of becoming a better reader probably won't work, and it will also be boring. If you don't think of yourself as someone who likes to read, think of topics you're interested in and curious about, and seek out related books and magazines. If you hate English class but love chemistry, for example, you might want to check out a magazine like *Scientific American*, which covers current scientific news in ways accessible to non-experts.

This process will help you become familiar with the kind of writing common in the recently published, wide-audience articles from which the PSAT draws its passages. More importantly, though, you'll be developing your interests and broadening your worldview.

You can also ask librarians or other trusted adults for recommendations. They can help you find a book related to something you're interested in, and they can often help you figure out what else you might like based on what you've enjoyed in the past. The specific things you read are less important than staying focused and aware while you're reading. If something in a book has an emotional effect on you, try to notice some things that author did that contributed to that effect.

INTRODUCTION TO THE WRITING TEST

Writers aim to make their writing as clear and effective as possible while following the standard rules of written English. Revision is an essential part of this process. The PSAT Writing and Language Test asks you to revise and edit texts about a variety of topics. You will identify and correct grammatical errors, as well as revise passages to better convey the authors' ideas.

Let's take a look at some information about the Writing section.

APPROACHING THE WRITING TEST
PART 1

THE STRUCTURE OF THE TEST

The new PSAT Writing Test is made up of four passages and 44 multiple choice questions. There is no essay. You will have 35 minutes to read the passages and answer the questions in this section. This means that you will have on average just under nine minutes to get through each passage and its accompanying questions. Don't worry if this seems like a small amount of time—the passages aren't long, and most of the questions are brief.

Each question corresponds to a number placed at a specific point in the passage. Unlike on the Reading Test, where the questions follow the full passage, on the Writing Test the questions and the passages are presented side-by-side. This means no flipping back and forth to locate the spot a question is asking you to consider!

PASSAGE TYPES

The passages on the Writing Test may be similar to essays you have encountered in school. Each Writing Test will include four different passages, one on each of the following topics: careers, social studies, humanities, and science.

- **Careers passages** usually present new trends or debates in major fields of work, such as health care, technology, or business.
- **Social studies passages** discuss figures, movements, and events from history, or topics in the social sciences. These social science topics might be drawn from anthropology, psychology, economics, or other fields in the social sciences.
- **Humanities passages** consider topics in the arts and letters, including figures and trends in fine art, music, dance, poetry, and prose.
- **Science passages** examine ideas, inventions, and discoveries in the natural sciences, which include earth science, biology, chemistry, and physics.

Each passage will be 400-450 words in length, broken up into paragraphs. The four passages together will add up to 1,700 words. At least one passage will also contain an informational graphic. The graphic may be a table, graph, or chart that conveys information that is related to the passage topic.

GENERAL TIPS

- **Read every sentence.** Every sentence is important! Even if sentences don't include question markers, they may give you valuable information that you will use to answer the questions.

- **Work on one passage at a time**. Make sure you attempt all questions for a passage before moving on. Because the questions are presented alongside the passage, it's easiest to answer them as you're reading. If you're not sure about a question, you can circle it in your test booklet and enter a guess on your answer sheet. That way, you can easily go back to the question if you have extra time to check your answers.

- **Don't worry about unfamiliar topics.** No matter what type of passage you are reading, you may see technical language you don't know. Don't worry! The Writing Test doesn't require any outside information about the topics in the passages. However, you will be expected to use the information the author gives you to decide whether an argument is logical, whether more facts are needed, and whether the ideas and grammar are sound.

QUESTION TYPES
PART 2

The Writing Test is essentially a test of your editing skills. As you read, you'll be asked to consider whether to make certain revisions to the passage. These revisions fall into two categories: Standard English Conventions and Development of Ideas.

STANDARD ENGLISH CONVENTIONS

The passages in the Writing and Language Test contain errors. Standard English Conventions questions will ask you to address underlined portions within the passages, determine if there is an error within each portion, and select answer choices that improve the sentences and passages as a whole.

Here is an example of what a question might look like:

The opera singer Jenny Lind is often considered one of the first true celebrities. When she first arrived in the United States, thousands of **1** exotic fans gathered to greet her with tossed flowers and live music.

A) NO CHANGE

B) ecstatic

C) extrinsic

D) exacting

The first answer choice (NO CHANGE) indicates that the underlined portion of the passage shouldn't be changed. The second, third, and fourth answer choices provide different versions of the underlined portion of the passage. This question is asking you to select the best option for the underlined portion of the sentence, either by replacing it with one of the alternate versions provided, or by leaving it as it is. Not every question will have NO CHANGE as an answer choice. For this question the correct answer is (B).

Standard English Conventions might ask about one word, as in the example above, or about a phrase, in which case the alternate answer choices will typically have more than one word as well. Either way, it should always be your goal to select the *best* option.

ANSWERING THE QUESTIONS

- **Use the Process of Elimination.** Even if you can't tell right away if there is an error in an underlined section or anticipate what the correct version would be, you can knock out answer choices that you know are incorrect. You can then compare the options you have left to select the best answer.

- **Check your answer**. Once you select an answer, you should go back to the passage and test your choice. Replace the underlined section with the answer you chose and re-read the new sentence. Doing this will ensure that the sentence is now the best version.

- **Don't be afraid to choose "no change."** Many students are hesitant to pick (A) because it seems "too easy." However, there *are* portions of the passage that are already in their best form and will need no correction. If you think that the portion is best unchanged, then it probably is! Go ahead and bubble in (A) NO CHANGE as your answer.

- **Guess if you have to**. As you learned in the introduction, there is no penalty to guessing on the new PSAT, so you should always guess if you don't know the correct answer. You can improve your chances of guessing correctly by using the process of elimination. You are much more likely to guess correctly when choosing between two answer choices than among four!

GRAMMAR

Standard English Conventions questions will test your understanding of grammatical rules and English conventions for language use and punctuation. If you are unfamiliar with grammatical terms, do not worry—the test will never explicitly ask about grammar. However, you will demonstrate your practical understanding of how English works through the choices you make as you correct the errors in the passage.

The Ivy Global New SAT Guide contains a detailed explanation of grammatical terms and rules. We won't go into the complete explanation here, but we will go over common grammar errors and harder grammar errors below. The following chart gives examples of the terminology that we will be referencing while explaining the errors that follow:

Term	Examples
Parts of Speech	Noun, pronoun, verb, adjective, adverb
Noun	<u>Seagulls</u> like to eat bread.
Concrete Noun	I baked too many <u>cookies.</u>
Abstract Noun	The soldiers showed great <u>bravery</u>.
Proper Noun	<u>Florida</u> is warm all year round.
Possessive Noun	Can I go to <u>Mark's</u> house?
Pronoun	<u>They</u> brought flowers from the garden.
Subject Pronoun	<u>We</u> saw Anisha at the party.
Object Pronoun	Anisha saw <u>us</u>, too.
Antecedent	My <u>sister</u> says <u>she</u> is scared of heights.
Verb	She <u>designs</u> wedding gowns.
Action Verb	We <u>drive</u> to New York every year.
Linking Verb	Mona <u>is</u> a wonderful actress.
Adjective	Jorge is a <u>good</u> actor.
Adverb	Jorge performed <u>well</u>.
Direct Object	Please hand Liam the <u>pencil.</u>
Indirect Object	Please hand <u>Liam</u> the pencil.
Preposition	The bat is still <u>in</u> the cave.
Object of the Preposition	The bat is still in the <u>cave.</u>
Present Tense	The band <u>plays</u> only cover songs.
Past Tense	We <u>clapped</u> when the curtain closed.
Imperfect Past Tense	The journalist <u>was searching</u> for a story.
Present Perfect Tense	Michael <u>has played</u> tennis for years.
Past Perfect Tense	I wasn't hungry because I <u>had eaten</u> earlier.
Past Participle	They have already <u>gone</u> to the store.
Future Tense	The President <u>will speak</u> at noon.
Active Voice	The chemicals <u>reacted</u> immediately.
Passive Voice	She <u>was discovered</u> by the detective.
Independent Clause	<u>Pigs can fly</u>, so you better watch your head.
Dependent Clause	<u>When pigs can fly</u>, the skies will be a scary place.
Conjunction	We bought ham <u>and</u> cheese.

Subordinating Conjunction	<u>Even though</u> she lost, we had a party.
Coordinating Conjunction	She practices a lot, <u>but</u> she never gets better.
Conjunction Pairs	<u>Neither</u> my sister <u>nor</u> my brother found out.
Fragment	Although he said he would
Phrase	Feeling happy
Run-on	You should take an umbrella it's raining.
Comma Splice	I am a calm person, I am not when I fly.
Subject-Verb Agreement	<u>Quinn and her sister are</u> at the pool.
Pronoun Agreement	<u>Each student</u> should say <u>his or her</u> name.
Conditional Sentence	If you study hard, you will succeed!
Parallel Structure	We enjoy jogging, hiking, and swimming.
Misplaced Modifier	Rushing to work, a bicycle hit Ron.
Logical Comparison	Timmy's bike is faster than Donald's bike.
Idiom	The Senator is <u>opposed to</u> the bill.

COMMON GRAMMAR ISSUES

Fragment: a set of words or a clause that cannot stand on its own, but that a writer has tried to use as a complete sentence

    ✗ Emma didn't show up until 9 PM. <u>Even though she said she'd arrive at 7.</u>

    ✓ Emma didn't show up until 9 PM<u>, even though she said she'd arrive at 7.</u>

Run-on sentence: when two independent clauses are combined without proper conjunctions or punctuation

    ✗ My cat is very mischievous she likes to climb where she's not supposed to be.

    ✓ My cat is very mischievous; she likes to climb where she's not supposed to be.

    ✓ My cat is very mischievous and likes to climb where she's not supposed to be.

    ✓ My cat is very mischievous. She likes to climb where she's not supposed to be.

Comma splice: when a comma is used to separate two independent ideas that could be separate sentences

    ✗   My dog is very obedient, she always sits when we tell her to sit.

    ✓   My dog is very obedient; she always sits when we tell her to sit.

    ✓   My dog is very obedient and always sits when we tell her to sit.

    ✓   My dog is very obedient. She always sits when we tell her to sit.

Subject-verb agreement: a verb must be in the correct form, given the number (singular or plural) of the noun

    ✗   The artist in the studio by the warehouse full of robots <u>draw</u> all day.

    ✓   The artist in the studio by the warehouse full of robots <u>draws</u> all day.

Pronoun agreement: pronouns must have the same number and gender as the nouns to which they refer (their antecedents)

    ✗   If <u>one changes</u> pronouns midsentence, <u>you are</u> doing it wrong.

    ✓   If <u>you change</u> pronouns midsentence, <u>you are</u> doing it wrong.

    ✓   If <u>one changes</u> pronouns midsentence, <u>one is</u> doing it wrong.

Verb tense: verbs in a sequence must be in the correct tense and voice

    ✗   If you <u>study</u> more, you <u>would get</u> better grades.

    ✓   If you <u>study</u> more, you <u>will get</u> better grades.

    ✓   If you <u>studied</u> more, you <u>would get</u> better grades.

    ✓   If you <u>had studied</u> more, you <u>would have gotten</u> better grades.

HARDER GRAMMAR ERRORS

Parallel structure: parts of a sentence that correspond with each other should have the same grammatical structure

- ✗ After a long day, I like listening to music, reading, and <u>to talk</u> with friends.
- ✓ After a long day, I like listening to music, reading, and <u>talking</u> with friends.

- ✗ On Andrea's vacation she would tour monuments, she would commune with nature, and <u>expensive knick-knacks would be purchased</u>.
- ✓ On Andrea's vacation she would tour monuments, she would commune with nature, and <u>she would purchase expensive kick-knacks</u>.

- ✗ Whether you <u>fight</u> with Ron or <u>gave</u> him the silent treatment, you're going to have to resolve the argument eventually.
- ✓ Whether you <u>fight</u> with Ron or <u>give</u> him the silent treatment, you're going to have to resolve the argument eventually.
- ✓ Whether you <u>fought</u> with Ron or <u>gave</u> him the silent treatment, you're going to have to resolve the argument eventually.

Misplaced modifiers: phrases or clauses that are separated from the words they are meant to describe, creating ambiguities or mistaken meanings

- ✗ Seasoned with many spices, Sam's mouth burned when he ate a bite of the curry.
- ✓ Sam's mouth burned when he ate a bite of the curry, which was seasoned with many spices.
- ✓ Seasoned with many spices, the curry burned Sam's mouth when he ate a bite of it.

LOGICAL ORDER

Within a paragraph, sentences should be organized in a logical order to help the reader follow the author's train of thought. When sentences are presented out of order, the thoughts seem jumbled, and it can be hard to figure out what the author is trying to say.

On the Writing Test, you will be asked to relocate, add, or remove sentences to improve the logical order of the paragraph. In order to answer these questions, you should first identify what the sentence is doing in the paragraph. Is it a main point, evidence, an example, or a conclusion? Once you know what the sentence accomplishes, you will be able to determine the best location for it within the paragraph.

PRECISION

Some questions on the Writing Test will ask you to choose which word or phrase best completes a sentence. To do so, you should first try to figure out what the writer is trying to say, then select the most precise word. Choosing the most **precise** word means choosing the one that is most appropriate in the context of the paragraph. Your goal should always be to choose the right word for what the author means to say.

CONCISION

Other questions will require you to make the author's phrases or sentences more concise. **Concise** phrases and sentences give the most information in the fewest words possible. The most concise option is not always the shortest, however. Sometimes when you make a sentence too short, you lose words that add meaning to the sentence. A concise answer will give all the same information as the original, just in fewer words. Generally on the PSAT, concision questions will include words that are redundant, meaning that they say something that has already been said.

- ✗ They had an annual celebration every year.
- ✓ They had an annual celebration.
- ✓ They had a celebration every year.

Because "annual" means "every year," you don't need to include both of them in the sentence to get across the idea. We've shown you two equally correct ways to fix that; on the PSAT, a multiple choice test, only one answer will fix the problem without introducing a new one.

STYLE AND TONE

An author can also express his or her ideas effectively using proper style. **Style** involves the words, phrases, and information the author chooses to include depending on the purpose of the passage. Style can refer to the way the author writes a sentence, a group of sentences, or the passage as a whole. Significant deviations from the author's style of choice are distracting and take away from the passage's effectiveness.

Authors also develop a specific **tone**, or attitude, throughout the passage. For example, an author can have an authoritative tone when writing as an expert, or a disapproving tone if he or she is arguing against a proposition. On the Writing Test, you will not be asked to identify a word that describes the author's tone. Instead, you'll be asked to revise sentences or phrases so that they match the tone of the rest of the passage.

The passages on the Writing Test are generally examples of informative writing: they serve primarily to give the reader new information. Even passages that do advance a particular argument do so in a way that avoids pointed language. This means that their tones are fairly neutral, so you can eliminate answer choices that sound particularly emphatic or emotional. They are written in a professional, polished style, so avoid language that is casual or conversational.

GRAPHICS

Some passages are accompanied by **graphical representations** of information, which include graphs, charts, or tables. When passages contain a graphic, it will be your job to choose the answer that best synthesizes the information from the graphic with the information presented in the passage. Here is an example of a kind of graphic you might see on the PSAT:

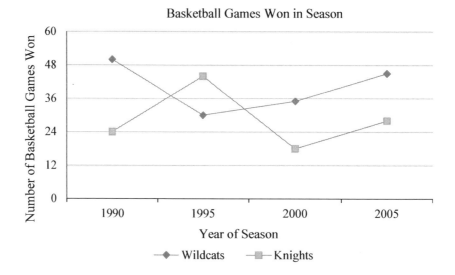

Basketball Games Won in Season

You can use the following checklist of questions to make sure you're properly reading a graph, chart, or table on the Writing Test.

✓ *What are the titles?*

Titles tell you what the graphic is talking about. Titles may tell you who the data is about, what was measured, or when the data was collected. Be sure to read the titles first to make sure you know what the graphic is about.

✓ *On a graph, what are the axes?*

The two major vertical and horizontal lines on a graph are its **axes**. Axes tell you what two things the graph is measuring—the **variables**. Axes may represent time, quantities, prices, or numbers of people. After looking at the title, make sure to find the axes and locate what is being measured in the graph.

✓ *What are the units?*

Units tell you how the graphic is measuring the variables. They are usually located next to or underneath titles or axes. We use units for numbers (hundreds, thousands, or millions), but also for things like temperature (Fahrenheit or Celsius). You shouldn't assume that units will be in the most common form, so always check what units the graphic is using. The units used in the graphic must be the same as in the correct answer choice. If not, you should check to make sure they were converted correctly.

To represent large numbers without cluttering a graphic, authors may use different units to show the same information. For example, if the data is in thousands, the author may use the unit "thousands" to show that without changing the numbers on the graphic itself. In this case, "1" would really mean "1,000."

✓ *Is there a legend?*

Some graphs and charts have a legend. The **legend** tells you what different colors, shadings, shapes, or lines represent. Legends are often located on the bottom or side of the graphic. You should locate the legend before you look at the data so you can correctly interpret the information presented.

Numbers in graphics are usually straightforward, but there are a few things you'll want to remember:

Totals and parts: Charts and tables will sometimes give you information about many groups. For example, pie charts may break up one large group into many subgroups and present numerical information about the subgroups. Tables may also present information about large groups and smaller subgroups or totals and parts. It is important to notice what the groups represent in a table.

Here is an example of a pie chart:

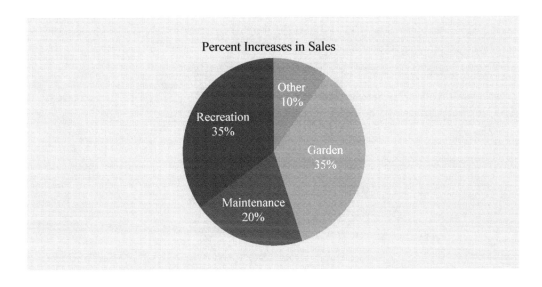

Be careful not to make assumptions: When two variables increase in number, you cannot assume they are related or that one causes the other. For example, a graph may show that both test scores and candy bars sold in the cafeteria increased by fifty this month. You cannot assume that eating candy bars caused the higher test scores (even though you might want to!).

Percentages: Percentages are another way to write fractions, or parts of a whole, and sometimes the author will use them to relay information. In graphs, percentages are often used to show changes, like increases or decreases. There are a few important things you want to remember about percentages:

- Percentages and numbers are different. Percentages represent a part of a total, but the total does not have to be one hundred. You know that having 10% is not the same as having ten, but this can be easily misinterpreted on graphs.
- In graphics that represent percentage increases or decreases, you cannot make assumptions about the numbers or totals without additional information.
- Large percentages do not always mean large numbers. For example, 90% may seem like a large percentage, but 90% of 10 is only 9. Likewise, large numbers do not always mean large percentages. For example, 800 may seem like a large number, but 800 is only 1% of 80,000.

Some of the graphics will be charts demonstrating the relationships between elements mentioned in the passage. Give yourself a moment to understand what the images portray and how they are organized.

Take your time, relate the information in the graphic to the information from the passage, and you'll be just fine.

CULTIVATING GOOD WRITING SKILLS
PART 3

The key to becoming a better writer is to read widely. Writing Test questions asking about style and tone are essentially asking you to decide whether particular words or phrases belong in a specific style of writing. However, you can't make that distinction if you haven't been exposed to different types of writing.

If an answer choice sounds like it belongs in an email rather than in a professional magazine, it's probably not correct. There are strategies you can develop to help you decide between two seemingly plausible answers, but what will really increase your score is becoming familiar with the kind of writing that appears on the Writing Test: informative writing aimed at adults.

Reading articles in newspapers and general-interest magazines—many of which can be found online—will make you more sensitive to subtle decisions writers make to convey a particular tone. This will fine-tune your inner gauge of what "sounds right" for the Writing Test, something that will also help you answer easier grammar questions quickly, leaving you more time to be careful with the trickier ones.

The other thing that will improve your writing is practice. When you have to write something for homework, look at it as an opportunity to improve your writing skills. You can practice editing your own sentences by looking out for errors you might make while working quickly. If your teachers give you corrections on your grammar, don't just glance at them and move on; make sure you understand the reason for the correction, and if you don't, see if you can ask your teacher after class.

Section 7

Introduction to the Math Test

In this section, we'll go over the format of the two sections of the Math Test so you know what to expect. Then, we'll talk about some general problem-solving techniques for different types of math problems, as well as strategies that will help you on the PSAT specifically. We'll also go over what kinds of math topics the PSAT tests so you can see what you need to master in order to maximize your score. Finally, we'll talk about some ways that you can build your mathematical skills gradually and durably, so you can approach math confidently on the PSAT and beyond.

APPROACHING THE MATH TEST
PART 1

THE STRUCTURE OF THE TEST

The Math Test on the PSAT/NSMQT has two parts. The first is the Calculator Not Permitted section, where you have to work out the answers to problems without the aid of a calculator. We'll refer to this as the No-Calculator section; it is 25 minutes long, and has 17 questions. Of those 17 questions, 13 will be multiple choice, with four options each. The other 4 questions will be student-produced response questions, or "grid-in" questions. For these, instead of selecting the right answer from a set of four choices, you'll fill in your own answers by bubbling in a set of numbers on a grid. We'll go over this process in the "Gridding-In" section below.

The second part of the Math Test is the Calculator section. On this part of the test, you are permitted to use a calculator. The Calculator section of the Math Test on the PSAT is 45 minutes long, and it has 31 questions. Of those 31 questions, 27 will be multiple choice, and the other 4 will be student-produced response questions. In both the Calculator section and the No-Calculator section, the student-produced response questions will appear at the end.

Every question on the Math Test will be worth one point, no matter how difficult or complicated. That's important to know when you're thinking about how to best manage your time during the test, which we'll discuss in more detail later.

KNOW THE DIRECTIONS

You will be given directions and reference information at the beginning of each math section of the SAT. The directions will tell you whether you can use a calculator and how long you have for that portion of the test—25 minutes for the No-Calculator section, or 45 minutes for the Calculator section.

The "Notes" section at the beginning of each math section will look similar to the one below. This box will tell you whether you can use a calculator on that section. It also gives you information about the figures and functions you will see and use on the test.

1. The use of a calculator **is / is not permitted**.

2. All variables and expressions used represent real numbers unless otherwise indicated.

3. Figures provided in this test are drawn to scale unless otherwise indicated.

4. All figures lie in a plane unless otherwise indicated.

5. Unless otherwise indicated, the domain of a given function f is the set of all real numbers x for which $f(x)$ is a real number.

The "Reference" section contains important formulas and facts. To use this information to your advantage, be familiar with what formulas are provided. Use this reference information when practicing for the PSAT. Remember that this information is only helpful if you know how to use it to solve problems!

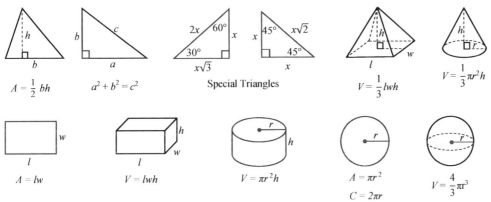

There are 360° in a circle.
The sum of the angles in a triangle is 180°.
The number of radians of arc in a circle is 2π.

GRIDDING IN

You'll use the same process to answer multiple choice questions in math as you do on the other parts of the test: pick the best answer from the set of choices given, and fill in the corresponding bubble on your answer sheet darkly and neatly, making sure not to make any stray marks.

Decimals must be as accurate as possible. If a decimal is longer than four characters, grid in the first four characters, including the decimal point, or it may be marked incorrect. For example, to grid 21/23 as a decimal, write .913 with no zero before the decimal point. (Note that the first column doesn't have a bubble for zero, anyway!) The response .91 may be scored as incorrect because it's less accurate than .913.

You do not have to follow rounding rules when shortening your answer. If you round, do so at the last digit that you can fit in the grid. 8.127 can be bubbled as 8.12 or as 8.13, but not as 8.1, which is less accurate. If in doubt, fill in as many digits as possible and do not round.

You don't need to reduce fractions as long as they fit in the grid. If your answer is $\frac{9}{12}$, you can grid it as 9/12, 6/8, or 3/4, or as the decimal .75.

Notice that the grid does not have an option for a minus sign. This means that the answers to student-produced response questions will always be positive or zero. If you get a negative number for an answer, either you have made a mistake or there are other possible answers. Check your work and rework the problem if necessary.

Math Test Strategies
Part 2

Reading Questions Carefully

On both math sections, make sure you read through the whole question instead of assuming you know what it's asking from the first few words.

If you see unfamiliar or difficult-looking material, stay calm and keep reading until the end of the question. There might be more information in the question that will help you to understand the problem, or you may find that the question is asking you to find something unrelated to the intimidating information.

If you still feel overwhelmed by a question after you've read the whole thing, make your best guess, circle the question in your question booklet, and come back to it if you have time. All questions are worth the same, so if you have to pick, it's better to spend your time on a question you feel comfortable tackling than on one that confuses you.

Problem Solving Strategies

The strategies below will help you solve the wide variety of questions you will see on the math sections. They will help you use your time and resources, such as your calculator and the test itself, to answer questions quickly while reducing your chance of making mistakes. They will also help you build good habits for mathematical reasoning.

1. Ask yourself, "What is this question asking me to solve?" This is especially important for word problems. Sometimes the wording of a question can be confusing, so make it simpler for yourself by summarizing in your own words exactly what the question is asking you to find. There might be times when you're not sure what this is, and in those cases, it can help to skip to the next step and then come back to identify what the question is asking.

2. Underline or circle key information you will need to use to solve the question. If a question is expressed only in numbers or symbols, you usually won't need to do

this, but it can help you isolate what's actually necessary in a word problem. This might be amounts, people, distances, measurements, units, or mathematical clue words like increase, decrease, more than, less than, or left over. This can be especially useful in a problem with a table, where you might be looking at several values but only need a few of them.

3. Draw a chart or diagram. This helps you visualize the problem and organize your information so you can take it all in at a glance.

4. Strategize the best way to solve the question. It's okay to spend a moment or two planning your approach instead of rushing in blindly and doing a bunch of work you might have to scrap. Think about all the information provided in the question and how it is related. Think about where you've seen this type of question before, and what methods you've used to solve similar types of questions. If there's a formula you think you can use, write it down to make sure you plug your values in correctly.

5. Check your answer. If you're making good time, you can take a moment to review your work right after finishing. Make sure you haven't made any careless errors in arithmetic, or mixed up your units, or forgotten to carry out a step. Also make sure you've answered what the question was looking for; for example, if the question asked you to solve for a perimeter, check to ensure that you didn't solve for area. If you're pressed for time, you can come back and do this when you've finished the section.

6. Don't forget to double-check your answer sheet as well as your math! It can help to circle the correct answer in your question booklet, so you can tell with one look whether you bubbled in the answer choice you meant to bubble in.

EDUCATED GUESSING

If you really have no idea how to solve a problem, you should always guess. Remember that you don't lose points for wrong answers on the PSAT, so you have nothing to lose by just picking a letter, ideally the same letter each time. Filling in a guess will also prevent answer sheet errors by ensuring that you have an answer for each question; this way, you can avoid accidentally shifting your answer choices and matching them to the wrong question.

However, even if you aren't sure how to solve a problem, you can often make a better guess or even find the right answer through the Process of Elimination. This is true across the PSAT, but math problems in particular often have specific restrictions that you can use to knock out incorrect answers.

Often, even without solving a problem, you can identify a range of numbers the answer must fall within. This might be very small: if you know that a number must fall between zero and one, for example, you can eliminate any answer choices that are greater than one, including any fractions where the numerator is greater than the denominator. Notice that you can knock those out without even evaluating them for their precise value!

Even a larger range can be helpful. You might not know anything about an answer except that it must be a positive value, but that can help you if there are any negative numbers listed as answer choices. If you know an answer has to be even, or divisible by five, you can eliminate answer choices to which those restrictions don't apply. If a word problem describes subtracting a particular amount from some real-world quantity, you know the original amount must be larger than the number being subtracted, because real amounts can't be negative.

PLUGGING IN ANSWER CHOICES

Sometimes it's easier or faster to find the correct answer by plugging the answer choices into the problem. This can save you from doing long or complicated calculations, especially on the Calculator section.

When you use this strategy, it's best to start with choice (B) or (C). Most answer choices are listed in increasing or decreasing numerical order, so if you start with (B) or (C), you may be able to eliminate multiple answers based on the results. For example, if the answers increase in value from (A) to (D) and you determine that choice (C) is too small, you can eliminate choices (A), (B), and (C), leading you straight to the correct answer—(D).

An exception to this guideline is when the problem asks you to find the largest (or smallest) value that satisfies a given condition. In those cases, it's better to start with the largest (or smallest) answer choice.

For example, if the answer choices increase in value from (A) to (D), and you are asked to find the largest value that produces a particular result, you won't learn much from plugging in (A): even if it does satisfy the condition, it might not be the largest value that does, so you still need to check other answer choices. If you start with (D) and go back up the list, however, you can stop as soon as you hit an answer that works, as it will be the largest number that satisfies your requirements.

REPLACING VARIABLES WITH NUMBERS

If you're more comfortable working with numbers than with variables, you can sometimes replace variables with numbers that will be easy to use. To avoid mixing up which number you've assigned to which variable, make sure to quickly jot down what you've replaced with what.

This approach can let you see quickly and with certainty which quantities are larger than others, or even how much larger they are, which is the kind of assessment the PSAT will often ask you to make. Some students also find it faster than manipulating variables. Even if you prefer manipulating variables, plugging in real numbers can be a good tool to double-check that your answer fulfills the requirements of a question.

When you're using this strategy, you'll want to use numbers that are simple and quick to work with, usually meaning relatively small whole numbers. However, avoid using the numbers 0, 1, or 2, because they have certain unique properties that mean they can often give "correct" solutions for more than one answer choice.

USING FIGURES

Any figure provided in the Math Test will be accurate unless noted otherwise. If an angle looks like a right angle, you can assume that it is one. It's also safe to assume other features are accurate, like parallel or perpendicular lines and relative angles or lengths. Charts, graphs, and gridded figures are always accurate.

Although you're not allowed to use a ruler, you can measure lengths by using the side of your answer sheet. Place the corner of the sheet at one point and mark the distance to another point in the question booklet. This strategy may help you eliminate answer choices or check your answer, although there will always be a way to solve these problems without measuring lengths. (Make sure you don't make any extra marks on your answer sheet by mistake!)

Some figures may not show all of the lines that you need to solve the problem. You should add any necessary lines or other marks as accurately as possible. For example, if you realize that a triangle has to be an isosceles triangle, you can mark the congruent sides with lines just like you'd see in a textbook. This can help you keep your thoughts straight, and it can sometimes even let you make a new connection by freeing up your mind from having to remember what you've already figured out.

You can also add in lengths or measurements as you figure them out, even if they're not the ones the question is asking for. Just make sure you use your problem-solving skills and stay focused on what you ultimately need to find.

If a figure is not provided, you might want to draw your own diagram. This is especially useful in questions asking about physical shapes, but figures may also be helpful for solving other types of problems. You might draw a number line, graph, or quick sketch of a situation. Keep your diagrams accurate, but simple—you're not being graded on this work, so it doesn't matter what it looks like except to the extent that you can read your own notes.

USING YOUR CALCULATOR

Every problem on the Math Test is designed so that it can be solved without a calculator. However, using a calculator on the section that allows you to do so can help you save time and avoid errors.

You must provide your own calculator. A scientific or graphing calculator is recommended. You cannot use calculators with keypads, styluses, touchscreens, internet access, cellular access, or power cords. You also cannot use calculators that can play or record audio, video, or images. Your calculator can't make noise, and you can't use a laptop, tablet, or phone as a calculator. For a list of acceptable calculators, see ivyglobal.com/study/links#calculator.

Make sure to practice using the calculator that you plan to bring to the PSAT so you are familiar with it during the test. Before the test, make sure your calculator is working properly and has fresh batteries, or bring a back-up calculator.

Don't rely too much on your calculator when you take the test. On some problems, using a calculator can slow you down. When starting a problem, think about how you will solve it and whether you need to use a calculator. Look for ways to simplify the problem that will make the calculation easier, such as factoring or reducing fractions.

Write down calculations and scratch work in the test booklet. This will help you avoid calculator errors and makes it easier to check your work and find errors. Also, remember that every problem can be solved without a calculator. If you find yourself doing complicated or tedious calculations, there is likely a simpler method to find the answer.

LOOKING FOR SHORTCUTS

None of the problems should require time-consuming calculations. If your solution strategy is long or complicated, look for a simpler method or a neat trick that can help you solve the problem more quickly. Also double-check to make sure you are solving for the correct variable or value. It's possible to get distracted by information that seems to demand complex math, when the question is actually asking you to find something much simpler. Stay focused on what you need to find.

There are often multiple ways to solve a problem, so look for shortcuts that will save you time and unnecessary work. Complicated-looking fractions or rational expressions can often be simplified so that working with them is easier and less demanding. Not only will this allow you to work through problems faster, but it will also cut down on chances for careless errors to creep in to your work.

CHECKING YOUR ANSWERS

When you check your work, you want to confirm that the value or variable you found was in fact what the problem was asking for. This is particularly important on problems that require multiple steps; make sure that your final solution was the final answer, and not an intermediate step on the way to what the question was asking for.

Watch out especially for answer choices that are factors, multiples, or other variations of your answer. You may have forgotten a final step or gone too far in your calculation.

For answers you've found by manipulating algebraic equations, plug your answer into the original equation to make sure it works. Mistakes in manipulating variables can result in an equation that's different from the one you were given to work with, leading you to an answer that might be true for the manipulated equation, but not true for the original question.

If you have time, it can also be a good idea to try to use a different process to find the answer—if you did make a mistake, it's unlikely that you would make a mistake with a different strategy that would result in exactly the same wrong answer. This can be especially valuable with grid-in problems.

Although on the PSAT you're not graded on your work the way you might be in class, when you do use the question booklet as scratch paper to work out calculations, it's still a good idea to do so neatly. This will help you while you're solving the problem by keeping it easy to identify what numbers and variables you're using and how they relate to each other. It will also come in handy when you're checking your work, since you'll be able to see right away the method you used previously.

If you solved a problem that relied on algebra by replacing a variable with a number, it's a good idea to carry out the math again with a different number. This will confirm that your answer is true mathematically, and not the result of a coincidental error.

Now that we've gone over important general strategies for the Math Test, we're going to talk briefly about the kinds of topics the Math Test will cover. This isn't a math review; the purpose of this section is to make sure you aren't caught off guard on test day, as well as to give you the chance to start catching up on any major topics you may feel a little rocky about.

MATH FUNDAMENTALS CHECKLIST

Math knowledge builds on itself, and the topics tested by the PSAT will be hard to tackle if you don't have a solid grounding in the basics. Before you begin studying for PSAT math, make sure you're comfortable with the topics listed below. If you're unsure of your skills in any of these areas, take some time to review them—it will make practicing the more complex math of the PSAT much easier.

- Factors and multiples

- Fractions
- Ratios
- Percentages
- Proportions
- Rates, including unit rate
- Exponents
- Radicals
- Scientific notation
- Basic geometry

MATH TEST QUESTIONS

PART 3

HEART OF ALGEBRA

8 questions in the Calculator section and 8 questions in the No-Calculator section will fall under the Heart of Algebra domain. These questions focus on your ability to analyze and work with linear equations and inequalities: in other words, equations and inequalities variables are only raised to a power of 1.

You can get a quick sense of how prepared you are for Heart of Algebra by checking your skills against this list. If there's a term you're unfamiliar with or a subject you feel you haven't mastered, try to study up on it before the exam. All of these topics, as well as those listed under the domains below, are covered in Ivy Global's New SAT Guide.

- Algebraic expressions
- Linear equations
- Inequalities
- Absolute values
- Functions
- Interpreting equations
- Graphing equations and inequalities
- Systems of linear equations

Heart of Algebra questions might ask you to solve for the value of a particular variable in an equation or inequality, or for a pair of variables in a system of equations or inequalities. They may ask you to determine the value of a constant or coefficient in an equation or system of equations; these systems may have no solution, one solution, or infinitely many solutions.

They also might ask you to relate linear equations or inequalities to particular contexts. Sometimes this will entail solving for a specific real-world amount. Other times, however, you'll be asked to create an equation or inequality to model a situation, or to interpret the meaning of a given equation or inequality.

Heart of Algebra questions may also contain graphical elements. You may be asked to match a linear equation to its correct graph, or to match a graph to the linear equation it represents. You might also have to identify key features of a graph, such as its intercepts and slope, from the equation or from a verbal description.

In general, Heart of Algebra questions require you to comfortably transition between the different possible meanings and expressions of linear equations and inequalities; you want to be able to think of any linear equation or inequality as an algebraic expression, in terms of a diagram or graph, and also as a model for a situation that might occur in the world.

PASSPORT TO ADVANCED MATH

6 questions in the Calculator section and 8 questions in the No-Calculator section will fall under the Passport to Advanced Math domain. Like Heart of Algebra questions, Passport to Advanced Math questions focus on your ability to solve and work through equations, text, graphics, and real life scenarios using algebraic concepts. One key difference is that Passport to Advanced Math questions will ask you to deal with quadratic and exponential functions and equations—that is, functions and equations where at least one variable is raised to a power that is greater or smaller than one.

You can get a quick sense of how prepared you are for Passport to Advanced Math by checking your skills against this list. If there's a term you're unfamiliar with or a subject you feel you haven't mastered, try to study up on it before the exam.

- Polynomial expressions
- Factoring polynomials
- Quadratic equations
- Quadratic functions and their graphs
- Exponential functions
- Systems of equations and inequalities
- Comparing expressions (linear, quadratic, and exponential)
- Applying functions to real-world problems

Passport to Advanced Math questions may ask you to solve for the value of a particular variable in quadratic equations. You may also be asked to manipulate the expression so that it reveals certain information, such as a minimum or maximum value, or the intercepts of the graph.

There will be questions which involve simplifying expressions or rewriting them through other methods. There may also be questions asking you to add, subtract, and multiply polynomial expressions and simplify the result. You might also be asked to rewrite rational expressions, or expressions that can be written as a fraction, which might involve performing some division as well as multiplication, subtraction, and addition. These types of questions require a solid grasp of the rules around manipulating expressions with variables, especially quadratic expressions.

As with Heart of Algebra questions, Passport to Advanced Math questions ask you to be comfortable moving from one form or meaning of an expression to another. You might be asked to identify the graph of a polynomial function using particular information, especially related to the zeroes of the function—the values of the variable for which the value of the whole function equals zero.

Passport to Advanced Math questions will also ask you to be comfortable with the use of function notation. They might ask you to create exponential functions—functions where the variable is in the exponent of a constant—to model a particular context. This requires you to understand what kinds of changes correspond to what kinds of functions, as well as the relationship between equations and their graphs.

PROBLEM-SOLVING AND DATA ANALYSIS

16 questions on the Math Test will fall under the Problem Solving and Data Analysis domain. All of them will be in the Calculator section. Problem Solving and Data Analysis questions will frequently ask you to create mathematical representations for and solve real-world problems, often drawing from science and social science. You will need to be able to understand and interpret what quantities and amounts mean in concrete contexts.

You can get a quick sense of how prepared you are for Problem Solving and Data Analysis by checking your skills against this list. If there's a term you're unfamiliar with or a subject you feel you haven't mastered, try to study up on it before the exam.

- Measurements and units, including unit conversions
- Properties of data, including reading graphs and interpreting tables
- Measurements of central tendency, including mean, mode, median, and standard deviation
- Statistics and probability
- Modeling and using data as evidence

These problems require fluency with ratios, rates, percentages, and proportional relationships, especially the ability to comprehend and use unit rates in problems. You will have to be able to carefully manage converting between different units. You may also need to manipulate the equation for density, understanding how it relates to mass and volume in order to calculate one of those three measurements. Also, the questions might ask you to make or use scale drawings to find answers.

There will also be Problem Solving and Data Analysis problems with graphic elements. You need to know how to get information from a scatterplot, as well as how to select and use the line or curve of best fit. You might also be asked to read bar graphs or pie charts, or to use information presented in tables to calculate frequencies, probabilities, or associations between variables.

Some problems will ask you to work with statistical tools. This could include calculating the mean, median, mode, and range of a set of data, or it might involve using those measures to compare two different sets of data. Comparison questions might also ask about standard deviation, margins of error, or confidence intervals; you won't be expected to calculate them, but you might be asked to interpret them in a specific context. You might also need to use data to make inferences about the population the data describes or to evaluate whether given inferences are warranted by the data presented.

ADDITIONAL TOPICS IN MATH

1 question on the Calculator section and 1 question on the No-Calculator section will fall under the domain of Additional Topics in Math. These might include geometric problems involving volume, trigonometric ratios, the Pythagorean theorem, radians, arc length, chord length, sector areas, circles in the coordinate plane, congruence, and similarity.

BECOMING A GOOD MATHEMATICIAN
PART 4

Your best bet for developing your mathematical skills is, of course, your math class. Make sure you take good, clear notes—even if you have a textbook, writing by hand can help you remember and make connections between the topics and methods you're learning about. Translating what you learn in class into language that's comfortable for you will help you learn it more completely and review it more quickly.

It's also important to have a strong approach to math. Sometimes, you can get through homework and even tests by just memorizing a series of facts and formulas, but over time this isn't the best way to learn. When you learn something new in math, really try to understand why it's true, well enough that you can explain it in your own words without looking at your notes.

Your textbook will often have explanations for the concepts it's describing, so don't just skip these to get straight to the point. The real point in math is the way concepts build on one another, which means connections are everywhere. The more you focus on those connections, instead of seeing math as a set of separate facts, the easier and more interesting math will become. The PSAT will reward the kind of deep understanding that comes with seeking the "why" behind formulas and rules—and so will the upper-level math you encounter in college or beyond.

Chapter 2
Practice Tests

PRACTICE TEST 1

PSAT

Directions

- Work on just one section at a time.
- If you complete a section before the end of your allotted time, use the extra minutes to check your work on that section only. Do NOT use the time to work on another section.

Using Your Test Booklet

- No credit will be given for anything written in the test booklet. You may use the test booklet for scratch paper.
- You are not allowed to continue answering questions in a section after the allotted time has run out. This includes marking answers on your answer sheet that you previously noted in your test booklet.
- You are not allowed to fold pages, take pages out of the test booklet, or take any pages home.

Answering Questions

- Each answer must be marked in the corresponding row on the answer sheet.
- Each bubble must be filled in completely and darkly within the lines.

    Correct ●   Incorrect Ⓐ ⊗ ⊘ ⓐ
                                ✪ ⓑ ⊜ ⊛

- Be careful to bubble in the correct part of the answer sheet.
- Extra marks on your answer sheet may be marked as incorrect answers and lower your score.
- Make sure you use a No. 2 pencil.

Scoring

- You will receive one point for each correct answer.
- Incorrect answers will NOT result in points deducted. Even if you are unsure about an answer, you should make a guess.

**DO NOT BEGIN THIS TEST
UNTIL YOUR PROCTOR TELLS YOU TO DO SO**

Download printable answer sheets, answer keys, and Excel scoring sheets from:

ivyglobal.com/study

Section 1

Reading Test

60 MINUTES, 47 QUESTIONS

Turn to Section 1 of your answer sheet to answer the questions in this section.

DIRECTIONS

Every passage or paired set of passages is accompanied by a number of questions. Read the passage or paired set of passages, then use what is said or implied in what you read and in any given graphics to choose the best answer to each question.

Questions 1-10 are based on the following passage.

This passage is adapted from Claire Cain Miller, "Where Young College Graduates Are Choosing to Live." © 2014 by *The New York Times Company*.

When young college graduates decide where to move, they are not just looking at the usual suspects, like New York, Washington and San Francisco.
Line Other cities are increasing their share of these
5 valuable residents at an even higher rate, led by Denver, San Diego, Nashville, Salt Lake City, and Portland, Ore. And as young people continue to spurn the suburbs for urban living, more of them are moving to the very heart of cities—even in
10 economically troubled places like Buffalo and Cleveland. The number of college-educated people age 25 to 34 living within three miles of city centers has surged, up 37 percent since 2000, even as the total population of these neighborhoods has slightly
15 shrunk.

Even as Americans over all have become less likely to move, young, college-educated people continue to move at a high clip—about a million cross state lines each year, and these so-called
20 "young and restless" don't tend to settle down until their mid-30s. Where they end up provides a map of the cities that have a chance to become future economic powerhouses.

About 25 percent more young college graduates
25 live in major metropolitan areas today than in 2000, which is double the percentage increase in cities' total population. All the 51 biggest metros, except Detroit, have gained young talent, either from net migration to the cities or from residents graduating
30 from college.

Denver has become one of the most powerful magnets. Its population of the young and educated is up 47 percent since 2000, nearly double the percentage increase in the New York metro area.
35 And 7.5 percent of Denver's population is in this group, more than the national average of 5.2 percent and more than anywhere but Washington, the Bay Area, and Boston. Denver has many of the tangible things young people want, economists say, including
40 mountains, sunshine and jobs in booming industries like tech. Perhaps more important, it also has the ones that give cities the perception of cultural cool, like bike-sharing. Other cities that have had significant increases in a young and educated
45 population and that now have more than their share include San Diego, Baltimore, Pittsburgh, Indianapolis, Nashville, Salt Lake City, and Portland.

At the other end of the spectrum are the cities
50 where less than 4 percent of the population are young college graduates. Among those, Detroit

CONTINUE →

lost about 10 percent of this group, while Providence gained just 6 percent and Memphis 10 percent. Atlanta, one of the biggest net gainers of

55 young graduates in the 1990s, has taken a sharp turn. Its young, educated population has increased just 2.8 percent since 2000, significantly less than its overall population. It is suffering the consequences of overenthusiasm for new houses

60 and new jobs before the crash, economists say.

How many eventually desert the city centers as they age remains to be seen, but demographers predict that many will stay. They say that could not only bolster city economies, but also lead to

65 decreases in crime and improvements in public schools. If the trends continue, places like Pittsburgh and Buffalo could develop a new reputation—as role models for resurgence.

Percent Change in the Number of College Graduates aged 25 to 34, from 2000 to 2012

Houston	50%
Nashville	48%
Denver	47%
Austin	44%
Portland	37%
Washington	36%
Buffalo	34%
Baltimore	32%
Los Angeles	30%
Pittsburgh	29%
St. Louis	26%
New York	25%
Top 51 metro areas, average	25%
Minneapolis	21%
Chicago	17%
Boston	12%
San Francisco	11%
Memphis	10%
Providence	6%
Atlanta	3%
Cleveland	1%
Detroit	-10%

1

The passage primarily focuses on which of the following?

A) Why recent college graduates prefer urban over suburban living environments

B) Why most American cities are experiencing a significant influx of college-aged students

C) Which cities recent graduates are flocking to and why

D) Whether metropolitan areas will show a rebound in population growth in the near future

2

The author suggests that an increased population of young graduates will likely lead to which of the following in those cities?

A) Economic growth

B) Risk of overpopulation

C) Severe pollution

D) Increased jobs in technology

3

Which of the following provides the best evidence for the answer to the previous question?

A) Lines 7-11 ("And as ... Cleveland")

B) Lines 21-23 ("Where they ... powerhouses")

C) Lines 41-43 ("Perhaps more ... bike-sharing")

D) Lines 58-60 ("It is ... say")

CONTINUE

4

The author suggests that the reason for the demographic change in most cities is due to young graduates' desire to

A) escape more crowded centers such as New York and San Francisco.

B) save on living costs by moving to inexpensive urban centers.

C) pursue economic and recreational opportunities.

D) branch out from the more familiar territories of their youth.

5

Which choice provides the best evidence for the answer to the previous question?

A) Lines 1-3 ("When young … San Francisco")

B) Lines 38-41 ("Denver has … tech")

C) Lines 43-48 ("Other cities … Portland")

D) Lines 66-68 ("If the … resurgence")

6

As used in line 8, "spurn" most nearly means

A) reject.

B) despise.

C) jilt.

D) defy.

7

The primary purpose of lines 16-21 ("Even as … mid-30s") is to

A) warn that the current data on population demographics will soon be out of date.

B) cite a reason why this particular demographic makes for an intriguing study.

C) characterize younger generations as fickle and irresponsible.

D) suggest it is easier to study older and more settled populations.

8

Which of the following is NOT a reason the author gives for why Denver is an enticing city for young college graduates?

A) Its cultural attractions

B) Its terrain and weather

C) Its thriving economy

D) Its affordable housing

9

As used in line 64, "bolster" most nearly means

A) maintain.

B) encourage.

C) strengthen.

D) defend.

CONTINUE

10

It can reasonably be inferred from the graphic that

A) Houston has more recent college graduates than any other major American city.

B) New York and St. Louis have roughly the same percentage of college graduates relative to the rest of their populations.

C) the population of college graduates aged 25-34 of Cleveland and Atlanta are aging relatively slowly compared to the same demographic in other major metropolitan areas.

D) Minneapolis, Chicago, and Boston saw population growth of college graduates aged 25-34, but at slower rates than the national average.

CONTINUE

Questions 11-19 are based on the following passage.

Passage 1

Passage 1 is adapted from Beth Skwarecki, "Where Do Baby Sea Turtles Go?" © 2014 by *Scientific American*. Passage 2 is adapted from James Gorman, "Tracking Sea Turtles as They Swim for Their Lives." © 2014 by *The New York Times Company*.

After baby loggerhead turtles hatch, they wait until dark and then dart from their sandy nests to the open ocean. A decade or so later they return to spend their teenage years near those same beaches. What
5　the turtles do and where they go in those juvenile years has been a mystery for decades. Marine biologists call the period the "lost years."

Following the tiny turtles has proved to be difficult. Researchers tried attaching bulky radio
10　tags, but the devices impeded the turtles' ability to move. The size of the tags shrank over time, yet the batteries remained stubbornly large. Then Kate Mansfield, a marine biologist at the University of Central Florida, got the idea to go solar. She saw
15　that other wildlife researchers were tracking birds with small solar panels. So her team decided to use similar tags with a matchbook-size panel, bringing the weight down to that of a couple of nickels.

Mansfield's group tagged 17 turtles that ranged
20　from three to nine months old. The scientists then plopped them off the coast of Florida and into the Gulf Stream, which is part of the North Atlantic Gyre, a system of currents that flows clockwise up the U.S. East Coast. Bryan Wallace, a marine
25　biologist at Stratus Consulting and Duke University who was not involved in the work, said the study is likely to be remembered as a seminal paper in sea turtle biology.

"Based on long-standing hypotheses, we'd expect
30　that the turtles would remain in the outer gyre currents and head toward the Azores," an archipelago off Portugal, Mansfield says. As the team tracked subjects over a few months, however, it found the turtles did not stick to this itinerary.
35　Many of them swam into the center of the gyre,

where seaweed accumulates. The turtles forage in the seaweed and use it for shelter.

The turtles also traveled faster than predicted, reaching the waters off North Carolina within three
40　weeks. At that speed, they could easily reach the Azores in less than a year. Although that timeline agrees with estimates based on passive drifting, the turtles take many side trips, which means their actual speed of locomotion is impressive. Another surprise:
45　the tags' temperature sensors consistently read several degrees higher than the turtles' local water temperature, which suggests that the seaweed mats keep these cold-blooded reptiles warm, an important condition for growth.

Passage 2

50　When loggerhead turtles hatch on the beach of Boavista, the easternmost of the Cape Verde islands, they head for the water to begin what biologists call a swimming frenzy. The beach and coastal waters are full of predators, and the babies are tasty,
55　nutritious and defenseless. They need to reach ocean currents as quickly as they can, to be carried to less dangerous waters. This is the pattern of baby sea turtles in general, and scientists have had a good idea of what currents they ride. But they haven't had
60　a reliable way to track the turtles' swims and see exactly how they manage their first hours.

With the help of a new gadget called a nano-tag, a miniature acoustic device that weighs less than two-hundredths of an ounce, Rebecca Scott and
65　several colleagues for the first time got detailed records of the early hours of baby turtles, information that adds to understanding of this internationally endangered species. "We were able to track newly hatched turtles from the beach to the
70　open ocean," said Dr. Scott, a researcher at the Geomar Helmholtz Center for Ocean Research in Kiel, Germany. "We've always known they've been swept away by ocean currents, but this is the first time we've been in the sea with them."
75　She attached the tiny acoustic transmitters to 11 hatchlings on Boavista. Researchers then followed

CONTINUE →

the baby turtles in a boat for as long as eight
hours, listening to the pings sent by the
transmitters. The turtles swam as far as nine miles

80 to reach the open ocean. The initial swimming
frenzy stayed constant for 24 hours and declined
strongly the night of the second day. And after
that, the hatchlings slept at night and didn't swim.
"They are born knowing what they should do,"

85 Dr. Scott said.

11

Dr. Mansfield got the idea to use solar panels when
she

A) wanted to use a more environmentally-friendly
technology for her research.

B) was looking for ways to cut experimental
costs.

C) realized that they were being used successfully
in other branches of her discipline.

D) discovered that their use would likely secure
government funding for her work.

12

Which choice provides the best evidence for the
answer to the previous question?

A) Lines 11-12 ("The size ... large")

B) Lines 14-16 ("She saw ... panels")

C) Lines 20-24 ("The scientists ... Coast")

D) Lines 38-40 ("The turtles ... weeks")

13

The author of the first passage supports the
assertion that turtles swim faster than expected by

A) mentioning experimental results from a study
in North Carolina that support this theory.

B) extrapolating from a small measured segment
of the turtles' journey, including projected
detours.

C) creating a detailed map of the turtles' journey
while accounting for occasional bouts of
passive drifting.

D) using the radio tags to measure the real-time
pace of the turtles as they journey into the
water.

14

Which choice provides the best evidence for the
answer to the previous question?

A) Lines 8-9 ("Following the ... difficult")

B) Lines 29-32 ("Based on ... says")

C) Lines 41-44 ("Although that ... impressive")

D) Lines 44-49 ("Another surprise ... growth")

CONTINUE

15

Marine biologists' use of the phrase "lost years" (line 7) is primarily meant to convey

A) the gap in research on sea turtles before it was taken up by Dr. Mansfield and her team.

B) the long decades that sea turtles spend hibernating in the ocean after departing from their nests.

C) the unknown location and activities of sea turtles between their hatching as babies and return home as adults.

D) the lives of baby sea turtles which are attacked by predators on their way to the ocean and do not survive.

16

In lines 24-28, Dr. Wallace's attitude towards Dr. Mansfield's work might best be described as

A) skeptical.

B) overwhelmed.

C) patronizing.

D) impressed.

17

As used in line 42, "passive" most nearly means

A) idle.

B) unreceptive.

C) submissive.

D) apathetic.

18

Which of the following best describes the difference between the experiment described in Passage 1 and the experiment described in Passage 2?

A) Dr. Mansfield used solar-powered radio tags to track turtles, while Dr. Scott used nano-tags.

B) Dr. Mansfield had no issue tracking the turtles, while Dr. Scott struggled to do so.

C) Dr. Mansfield tracked adult turtles, while Dr. Scott tracked adolescent turtles.

D) Dr. Mansfield tracked turtles in an artificial environment, while Dr. Scott tracked them in their natural environment.

19

Both passages suggest that tracking sea turtles after they hatch will

A) help ensure the safety and permanence of this endangered species.

B) shed light on a little-researched period in the turtles' life.

C) aid researchers' understandings of the flow of ocean currents.

D) rejuvenate interest in this underappreciated organism.

CONTINUE

Questions 20-28 are based on the following passage.

This passage is adapted from G.K. Chesterton, *The Wisdom of Father Brown*, originally published in 1914.

The consulting-rooms of Dr. Orion Hood, the eminent criminologist and specialist in certain moral disorders, lay along the sea-front at Scarborough, in
Line a series of very large and well-lighted French
5 windows, which showed the North Sea like one endless outer wall of blue-green marble.

Dr. Hood paced the length of his string of apartments. His hair was heavily shot with grey, but growing thick and healthy; his face was lean, but
10 sanguine and expectant. Everything about him and his room indicated something at once rigid and restless, like that great northern sea by which (on pure principles of hygiene) he had built his home.

The door opened inwards and there shambled
15 into the room a shapeless little figure, the very embodiment of all that is homely and helpless.

The doctor regarded the newcomer with a restrained astonishment, not unlike that he would have shown if some huge but obviously harmless
20 sea-beast had crawled into his room. The newcomer regarded the doctor with that beaming but breathless geniality which characterizes a corpulent charwoman who has just managed to stuff herself into an omnibus. With an unimpaired smile on his
25 round face, he spoke simultaneously as follows:

"My name is Brown. Pray excuse me. I've come about that business of the MacNabs. I have heard, you often help people out of such troubles. Pray excuse me if I am wrong."

30 "I hardly understand you," replied the scientist, with a cold intensity of manner. "I fear you have mistaken the chambers. I am Dr. Hood, and my work is almost entirely literary and educational. It is true that I have sometimes been consulted by the
35 police in cases of peculiar difficulty and importance, but—"

"Oh, this is of the greatest importance," broke in the little man called Brown. "Why, her mother won't let them get engaged."
40 The brows of Dr. Hood were drawn down darkly, but the eyes under them were bright with something that might be anger or might be amusement. "And still," he said, "I do not quite understand."

"You see, they want to get married," said the
45 man with the clerical hat. "Maggie MacNab and young Todhunter want to get married. Now, what can be more important than that?"

At the last plea of the ingenuous priest a chuckle broke out of Dr. Hood from inside, and he threw
50 himself into an arm-chair in an ironical attitude of the consulting physician.

"Mr. Brown," he said gravely, "it is quite fourteen and a half years since I was personally asked to test a personal problem: then it was the case
55 of an attempt to poison the French President at a Lord Mayor's Banquet. It is now, I understand, a question of whether some friend of yours called Maggie is a suitable fiancée for some friend of hers called Todhunter. Well, Mr. Brown, I am a
60 sportsman. I will take it on. I will give the MacNab family my best advice, as good as I gave the French Republic and the King of England. I have nothing else to do this afternoon. Tell me your story."

The little clergyman called Brown thanked him
65 with unquestionable warmth, and began his recital:

"There is a very honest but rather sharp-tempered member of my flock, a widow called MacNab. She has one daughter, and she lets lodgings. At present she has only one lodger, the young man called
70 Todhunter; but he has given more trouble than all the rest, for he wants to marry the young woman of the house."

"And the young woman of the house," asked Dr. Hood, with huge and silent amusement, "what does
75 she want?"

"Why, she wants to marry him," cried Father Brown, sitting up eagerly. "That is just the awful complication."

"It is indeed a hideous enigma," said Dr. Hood.

CONTINUE

20

Why does Dr. Hood agree to hear Father Brown's case?

A) He pities the priest and wants to help him.

B) He is bored and the priest's plea amuses him.

C) His practice is failing and he needs the money.

D) He realizes the case is of utmost importance.

21

Which of the following provides the best evidence for the answer to the previous question?

A) Lines 32-33 ("I am … educational")

B) Lines 37-38 ("Oh, this ... Brown")

C) Lines 48-51 ("At the ... physician")

D) Lines 52-56 ("Mr. Brown … Banquet")

22

As used in line 2, "certain" most nearly means

A) particular.

B) unquestionable.

C) positive.

D) indisputable.

23

In lines 10-13 ("Everything about … home"), the author compares Dr. Hood and the ocean in order to

A) suggest elements of Dr. Hood's character.

B) highlight Dr. Hood's favorite natural landscape.

C) foreshadow the arrival of Father Brown.

D) hint at secrets Dr. Hood is hiding beneath the surface.

24

Which of the following best describes the initial reactions of Father Brown and Dr. Hood upon meeting?

A) Dr. Hood was delighted, while Father Brown was hesitant.

B) Dr. Hood was bemused, while Father Brown was apologetic.

C) Dr. Hood was surprised, while Father Brown was pleased.

D) Dr. Hood was frightened, while Father Brown was aggressive.

25

Why does Dr. Hood bring up his previous work on the poison attempt on the French President?

A) To prove his qualifications for the case

B) To contrast Mr. Brown's request with the significance of his usual cases

C) To show his work expands beyond the literary and educational

D) To suggest that they are all in danger

26

As used in line 65, "unquestionable" most nearly means

A) genuine.

B) dependable.

C) certain.

D) absolute.

CONTINUE

27

Dr. Hood's use of the phrase "hideous enigma" (line 79) most strongly suggests that he

A) believes the case to be unsolvable.

B) is humoring Father Brown.

C) finds this unimportant case distasteful.

D) doubts many of the facts of the case.

28

Which of the following provides the best evidence for the answer to the previous question?

A) Lines 64-65 ("The little ... recital")

B) Lines 68-72 ("At present ... house")

C) Lines 73-75 ("And the ... want")

D) Lines 76-77 ("Why, she ... eagerly")

CONTINUE

Questions 29-38 are based on the following passage.

This passage is adapted from Gretchen Reynolds, "How Music Can Boost a High-Intensity Workout." © 2014 by *The New York Times Company*.

Intense, highly demanding exercise has many health benefits and one significant drawback: it can be physically unpleasant, which deters many people from beginning or sticking with an intense exercise program. An encouraging new study, however, suggests that listening to music may nudge people into pushing themselves harder than they had thought possible.

Strenuous exercise, especially in the form of high-intensity interval training, has interested many scientists and exercisers in recent years. High-intensity intervals are brief bouts of hard, draining exercise interspersed with rest periods. Past studies have shown that 15- or 20-minute sessions of interval training improve people's fitness and reduce their risk for many chronic diseases as effectively as much longer bouts of moderate, continuous endurance training. In other words, high-intensity interval training promises a hefty fitness bang from a small time investment.

But as those of us who have experimented with this type of exercise quickly learn, that time, short as it may be, is punishing. Many people find the experience "aversive," said Matthew Stork, a graduate student at McMaster University in Hamilton, Ontario, who led the new study. Mr. Stork and his colleagues at McMaster, who have conducted many studies of high-intensity interval training, wondered if it would be possible to find ways to modify people's perceptions of how little they were enjoying the exercise. Immediately, they thought of music. Many past studies have found that listening to music changes people's experience of exercise, with most people reporting that listening to energetic songs makes a workout feel easier and less monotonous.

But those studies have generally involved standard endurance exercise, such as 30 minutes or so of continuous jogging or cycling. Few have examined the effect that music might have during intense intervals, in part because many exercise scientists have suspected that such training is too draining. The physiological noise bombarding people from their own muscles and lungs during intervals, many scientists have thought, would drown out the music, making any effect negligible.

But Mr. Stork was unconvinced. So he recruited 20 young, healthy adult volunteers, brought them into the lab, and had them follow a precise regimen. Using stationary bicycles, they completed four 30-second bouts of what the researchers call "all-out" pedaling, at the highest intensity that each volunteer could stand. Each 30-second bout was followed by four minutes of recovery time, during which the volunteers could pedal gently or climb off the bike and sit or walk about. Throughout the all-out intervals, meanwhile, the scientists tracked the volunteers' pedaling power output and asked them how hard the exercise felt. After that workout, the volunteers sat down and listed their favorite songs, which the researchers then downloaded and used to create custom playlists for each volunteer. Then each volunteer returned twice more to the lab, grunting through two additional sessions of the high-intensity intervals. During one, they listened to their chosen playlist. In the other, they did not listen to music.

Afterward, the researchers compared the riders' power outputs and reported feelings about the workout's difficulty. The volunteers all reported that the intervals had been hard. In fact, their feelings about the difficulty were almost identical, whether they had been listening to music or not. Interestingly, though, their power output had been substantially greater when they were listening to music. They were pedaling much more ferociously than without music, but they did not find that effort to be more unpleasant. The intensity increased but not the discomfort.

How music affects performance and perceptions during intense exercise remains unclear, Mr. Stork

CONTINUE

said, but it likely involves "arousal responses." The body responds to the rhythm of the music with a physiological revving that prepares it for
85 the demands of the intervals. People may also turn to music in hopes of ignoring their body's insistent messages of discomfort. Music cannot, of course, override those messages altogether, Mr. Stork pointed out. But it may mute them and
90 make you more eager to strain through another session of intervals, sweat and playlist streaming.

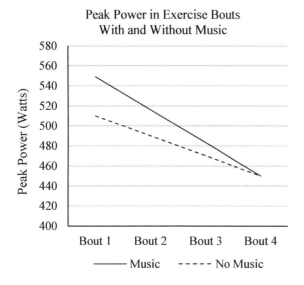

Peak Power in Exercise Bouts
With and Without Music

Mean Power in Exercise Bouts
With and Without Music

29

The author makes use of which of the following to support the passage's claims?

A) Anecdotal evidence from close friends

B) Research studies from credible sources

C) Polls from various groups of exercisers

D) Data from her own experiments

30

Based on the passage, which of the following statements would the author most likely agree with?

A) Music is more helpful during high-intensity interval training than in endurance training.

B) Music will likely increase the effectiveness, if not the ease, of high-intensity interval training.

C) More research on music and high-intensity interval training is needed before any conclusions can be drawn.

D) Music has a negligible effect on enjoyment and output in exercise.

31

Which choice provides the best evidence for the answer to the previous question?

A) Lines 47-49 ("So he ... regimen")

B) Lines 50-53 ("Using stationary ... stand")

C) Lines 74-76 ("Interestingly, though ... music")

D) Lines 87-89 ("Music cannot ... out")

CONTINUE

32

Which of the following best describes the author's attitude towards high-intensity interval training?

A) It is a good substitute for those without time for more rigorous exercise like long-distance endurance training.

B) It is a popular though dangerous form of exercise.

C) It is a difficult but highly beneficial form of exercise.

D) It is often unpleasant and thus not an ideal form of exercise.

33

Which choice provides the best evidence for the answer to the previous question?

A) Lines 1-5 ("Intense, highly ... program")

B) Lines 9-11 ("Strenuous exercise ... years")

C) Lines 43-46 ("The physiological ... negligible")

D) Lines 56-59 ("Throughout the ... felt")

34

According to the passage, how does Matthew Stork's research differ from most other research on exercise and music?

A) It focuses on high-intensity interval training.

B) It tests the effects of both fast-paced and slow-paced music on exercise.

C) It has research participants exercise on stationary bikes, while most research has them run on treadmills.

D) It allows participants to choose their music, while most other studies have pre-set playlists.

35

Which hypothetical situation is most analogous to adding music to a high intensity workout routine?

A) An engineer upgrades his workshop machinery to improve the quality of his work, but at a significant cost.

B) A construction worker uses a power tool that allows him to do more work, but is just as hard to use as a hand-tool.

C) A homeowner switches to more energy-efficient electricity providers in order to save on maintenance costs.

D) A writer listens to music while working to gain inspiration and get more pleasure out of her work.

36

As used in line 76, "ferociously" most nearly means

A) viciously.

B) intensely.

C) dreadfully.

D) brutally.

37

As used in line 89, "mute" most nearly means

A) deaden.

B) smother.

C) dampen.

D) silence.

CONTINUE

38

Information from the graph best supports which of the following statements?

A) Music affected peak performance more than average performance.

B) The difference in power for the two workouts increased with each bout.

C) The effects of music on exercise were strongest later in a workout.

D) Overall, music had no impact on performance.

CONTINUE

Questions 39-47 are based on the following passage.

The following is adapted from a speech given by Emma Goldman in 1917, as the United States was entering World War I. Goldman was a political activist and anarchist active in the early twentieth century. In this speech, entitled "Against Conscription and War," Goldman is responding to the conviction of two men for obstructing the draft.

Of course, friends, of course since the war was declared by a country in whose interest it is that the American boy shall be sacrificed it was not to the
Line interest of that country to put the war to a test and
5 therefore conscription had to be imposed upon you. Don't you know that during the Spanish-American War when the people believed in the war there was no need of asking the young men of the country, at the point of the bayonet and gun and club, to put on
10 an American uniform? They flocked to the war because they believed in it. And whether they were American citizens or were residents of America, the people of America were all willing to give their lives for something they considered right and just. But
15 because the people of America do not believe in this war, because the people of America have not been asked whether there shall be war, that is why they do not flock to the colors and that is why you in America are doing as the Russians used to do, as the
20 German Kaiser is doing, as all the Imperialistic tyrants are doing. But you are forgetting one thing, gentlemen of the law, you are driving a horse to water but you cannot compel him to drink. You will put the young manhood of America in the uniform,
25 you will drag them to the battlefield and into the trenches, but while they are there, there is going to be a bond of anti-militarism among the people of the world.

No, friends, you cannot compel human beings to
30 take human life, if you give them the chance to reason and to think, to investigate and to analyze.

And now we come down to the tragedy that was committed in the United States Court in the State of New York yesterday, when two boys were
35 sentenced. It is not only a tragedy because they were sentenced. Such things happen every day; hundreds, thousands of innocent working men are sent to the prison and the penitentiary, thousands of unfortunates throughout the world as well as here in
40 so-called free America and nobody ever hears anything about it. It is an ordinary, commonplace thing to do. But the tragedy of yesterday is in the fact that a Judge, supported as you have been told by your money, protected by public opinion, protected
45 by the President, the tragedy of it is that that Judge had the impudence and audacity to insult Kramer and Becker after he gave them the sentence of such horrible dimensions. Think of a man like that who sits there in judgment on other human beings. Think
50 what must be his character, what must be his mind, what must be his soul, if he can spit human beings in the face, only because he has got the power.

I wish to say here, and I don't say it with any authority and I don't say it as a prophet, I merely tell
55 you—I merely tell you the more people you lock up, the more will be the idealists who will take their place; the more of the human voice you suppress, the greater and louder and the profounder will be the human voice. At present it is a mere rumbling, but
60 that rumbling is increasing in volume, it is growing in depth, it is spreading all over the country until it will be raised into a thunder and people of America will rise and say, we want to be a democracy, to be sure, but we want the kind of democracy which
65 means liberty and opportunity to every man and woman in America.

CONTINUE

39

The tone of the passage is best described as

A) joyous.

B) frightened.

C) apathetic.

D) zealous.

40

Goldman is most likely addressing

A) a judge at the author's own trial.

B) a group of people at a protest.

C) an unsympathetic press.

D) a crowd of politicians she is seeking to sway.

41

Why did Goldman bring up the trial of the two workingmen?

A) She wanted to show how judges have too much power to determine sentences in America.

B) She hoped to convince her audience that not all anarchists are as troublesome as the two workingmen.

C) She offered the trial as proof of her claim that American authorities were acting tyrannically and oppressively.

D) She wished to raise funds and support for the defense of Kramer and Becker.

42

Which choice provides the best evidence for the answer to the previous question?

A) Lines 36-41 ("Such things ... it")

B) Lines 42-48 ("But the ... dimensions")

C) Lines 49-52 ("Think what ... power")

D) Lines 59-66 ("At present ... America")

43

Which of the following best represents Goldman's views on America's participation in WWI?

A) It is unacceptable because the American people do not believe in the cause.

B) It is unfortunate but necessary, since sacrifices must be made for peace.

C) It is unfair because the government cannot conscript individuals, who alone have the right to fight and bear arms.

D) It is welcome as long as individuals understand the reasons for their participation.

44

Which of the following provides the best evidence for the answer to the previous question?

A) Lines 6-10 ("Don't you ... uniform")

B) Lines 14-21 ("But because ... doing")

C) Lines 48-49 ("Think of ... beings")

D) Lines 53-59 ("I wish ... voice")

CONTINUE

45

As used in line 46, "audacity" most nearly means

A) rudeness.

B) fearlessness.

C) bravery.

D) gall.

46

Goldman condemns the judge in the passage mostly because he

A) condemned and then insulted two innocent people.

B) sentenced the two people without waiting for all the relevant facts.

C) assaulted the two people after the trial.

D) does not exhibit appropriate moral or spiritual values.

47

As used in line 57, "suppress" most nearly means

A) stifle.

B) conquer.

C) withhold.

D) control.

STOP

If you complete this section before the end of your allotted time, check your work on this section only. Do NOT use the time to work on another section.

Writing and Language Test

35 MINUTES, 44 QUESTIONS

Turn to Section 2 of your answer sheet to answer the questions in this section.

DIRECTIONS

Every passage comes with a set of questions. Some questions will ask you to consider how the writer might revise the passage to improve the expression of ideas. Other questions will ask you to consider correcting potential errors in sentence structure, usage, or punctuation. There may be one or more graphics that you will need to consult as you revise and edit the passage.

Some questions will refer to a portion of the passage that has been underlined. Other questions will refer to a particular spot in a passage or ask that you consider the passage in full.

After you read the passage, select the answers to questions that most effectively improve the passage's writing quality or that adjust the passage to follow the conventions of standard written English. Many questions give you the option to select "NO CHANGE." Select that option in cases where you think the relevant part of the passage should remain as it currently is.

Questions 1-11 are based on the following passage.

All of a Sudden: The Avalanche

The mountain air is still. The **1** gentle, call of a chickadee rings out into the clear evening. If there were any people on the mountain, they would certainly be able to see their breath—it's January, and it's cold.

Just a few hours ago, a snowstorm raged over the rocks and trees of northern Colorado, leaving fourteen inches of new snow over the mountain pass. This new snow settled on top of the **2** snowpack—the rest of the snow and ice from dozens of earlier storms and flurries adding new pressure to the already tenuous connection between a layer of ice and snow about eight feet down.

1

A) NO CHANGE
B) gentle call of a chickadee rings
C) gentle call, of a chickadee rings
D) gentle call, of a chickadee, rings

2

A) NO CHANGE
B) snowpack—the rest of the snow and ice from dozens of earlier storms and flurries, adding
C) snowpack, the rest of the snow and ice from dozens of earlier storms and flurries, adding
D) snowpack; the rest of the snow and ice from dozens of earlier storms and flurries, adding

CONTINUE

Suddenly, the snow below [3] give out. It breaks off from the icy layer underneath it and immediately starts pulling all the snow on top of it down the mountain. The early evening stillness is [4] toppled. This is a slab avalanche, beginning many feet under the surface of the snow and disturbing enormous chunks of snow and ice that tumble down the mountain. Within five seconds, the avalanche is moving at 130 kilometers per hour (80 miles per hour).

As the large chunks of snow fall, [5] they break into smaller and smaller pieces, as large chunks of rock might break up during rockslides. A cloud of ice particles rises high above the descending white mass. The avalanche instantly buries everything in its path. Over 200,000 cubic meters of snow are released and rapidly picking up speed—they reach 320 kilometers per hour (200 miles per hour) at their peak velocity.

[3]

A) NO CHANGE
B) will give
C) gives
D) gave

[4]

A) NO CHANGE
B) dismantled
C) shattered
D) impaired

[5]

Which of the following choices best improves the focus of the passage?

A) NO CHANGE
B) they break into smaller and smaller pieces.
C) they are like large chunks of rock breaking up during rockslides.
D) they break into smaller and smaller pieces, as large chunks of rock might break up during rockslides, which are often caused by rainstorms.

CONTINUE

[1] While visually dramatic, slough avalanches do little to disrupt the rest of the mountain's snow structure. [2] Had this been a slough (or "sluff") avalanche, starting on the surface of the snow and traveling down on top of the rest of the snowpack, it would have been far less powerful. [3] The slab avalanche, however, completely disrupts the snow underneath. [4] It is much more likely that a slab avalanche will tear down buildings and trees than **6** a slough avalanche. **7**

6

A) NO CHANGE
B) that a slough avalanche will do so.
C) the lesser strength of a slough avalanche.
D) the way slough avalanches behave.

7

For the sake of the logical progression of this paragraph, sentence 1 should be placed

A) where it is now.
B) after sentence 2.
C) after sentence 3.
D) after sentence 4.

CONTINUE →

[8] As it starts approaching the foot of the mountain, the avalanche [9] wanes in strength, and a runout zone formed where the snow and debris begin to spread out. Shortly thereafter the deposition zone [10] forms, where everything comes to rest.

8

A) NO CHANGE

B) Beginning its approach of the foot of the mountain,

C) As it approaches the foot of the mountain,

D) It approaches, and

9

A) NO CHANGE

B) waned in strength, and a runout zone forms

C) is waning in strength, and a runout zone formed

D) wanes in strength, and a runout zone forms

10

A) NO CHANGE

B) forms, the place where everything comes to rest.

C) forms, where everything comes to rest and stays.

D) forms, where everything comes to rest in a deposition zone.

CONTINUE

11 The whole event lasted less than a minute. Thankfully, there were no skiers today, otherwise they would have been buried under the immense white blanket left in the aftermath of the avalanche. After the last snow chunks settle, the cloud of icy particles also comes to rest. The night is clear and cold, and the air is still again.

11

Which choice most effectively establishes the main topic of the paragraph?

A) The avalanche was brief, but will have an impact on the flora and terrain of the mountainside for years to come.

B) Almost as abruptly as it began, the avalanche comes to a halt.

C) Many avalanches are caused when people dislodge snow while skiing or snowboarding.

D) The avalanche was mighty, imposing, and deadly.

CONTINUE

Questions 12-22 are based on the following passage.

The Pacific's First Explorers

Three thousand years ago, the islands of the Remote Pacific were completely uninhabited by human beings. Then, over the course of a few hundred years, the Lapita people explored and settled the islands over a spread of millions of square miles of the Pacific Ocean. They began in Papua New Guinea and **12** traveled east by journeying eastward in canoes. After a few generations, they had spread as far as Fiji and Polynesia. There were probably never more than a few thousand of **13** the Lapita people. They crossed uncharted waters, spread their language and culture, and left an enduring legacy.

12

A) NO CHANGE

B) traveled eastward

C) traveled in an eastward direction

D) traveled out on a journey to the east

13

Which of these options most effectively combines the sentences at the underlined portion?

A) the Lapita people, but they crossed

B) the Lapita people; they crossed

C) the Lapita people who crossed

D) the Lapita, but then the people crossed

14 Not overcrowded or lacking in resources, historians can only guess as to why the Lapita people originally left New Guinea. The most common conjecture is simply that they were curious about the world and had a sense of adventure. However, the Lapita also colonized the islands they discovered. They brought seedling plants on boats to develop their agriculture on new islands. **15** The Lapita also brought pigs, dogs, and fowl. Not only are the animals present on the islands today, but their bones are found in many archeological dig sites. The Lapita discovered and colonized hundreds of islands, sometimes settling in the interior of the islands and sometimes building houses on poles directly over the water in lagoons.

14

A) NO CHANGE

B) Historians, not overcrowded or lacking in resources, can only guess as to why the Lapita people originally left New Guinea.

C) Historians can only guess as to why the Lapita people, not overcrowded or lacking in resources, originally left New Guinea.

D) Historians can only guess as to why the Lapita people originally left New Guinea, not overcrowded or lacking in resources.

15

The writer wants to insert a sentence here to provide supporting evidence for the claim that the Lapita brought plants with them to new islands. Which choice best accomplishes this goal?

 A) Evidence suggests that the Lapita people enjoyed a varied diet of plants, fish, game, and meat from domesticated animals.

 B) Over-hunting on newly explored islands caused some animal species to go extinct, so food crops came in handy.

 C) Some plants present on the islands today are biologically incapable of spreading on their own, and must have been spread in this manner.

 D) The Lapita did not bring these plants along merely to eat on the voyage, but to propagate on new islands as food crops.

CONTINUE

[16] They decorated [17] there clay pots by pressing carved stamps into the wet clay before it dried. Archeologists recently discovered a Lapita cemetery in the northern Philippines containing sixty-two skeletons and a variety of pottery fragments. There, they discovered a clay pot burial urn with bird figurines around the top that the Lapita had modeled to appear as if [18] they were looking down at the human bones inside. This type of nuanced artistry [19] attests for a complex and imaginative culture.

16

Which choice most effectively establishes the main topic of the paragraph?

A) Lapita skeletons were found in an area called Efete.

B) Birds were sometimes a feature of Lapita art.

C) The Lapita are known for their distinctive pottery.

D) The Lapita's ritual burial practices provide clues about their religion and culture.

17

A) NO CHANGE

B) their

C) they're

D) they

18

A) NO CHANGE

B) the archeologists

C) the birds

D) those

19

A) NO CHANGE

B) attests of

C) attests to

D) attests

CONTINUE →

All of our knowledge about the Lapita comes from minimal clues; archeologists and historians glean what information they can from small pieces of pottery, obsidian flakes, animal bones, and geochemical data. **20** They hope to find new Lapita sites to increase the wealth of knowledge about these influential and adventurous people.

The **21** Lapitas' descendants are the more widely heard of Polynesians: the Hawaiians, the Tahitians, and the people of Easter Island. Their common language and culture were passed down from their Lapita ancestors, and they continued to spread the legacy of the original navigators as they spread further and further throughout the Pacific. **22** By the time Europeans arrived in the Pacific, every habitable island was already inhabited by the descendants of the Lapita.

20

A) NO CHANGE
B) They're hoping so much to find
C) They endeavor without rest to find
D) I hope they find

21

A) NO CHANGE
B) Lapita descendants
C) Lapita's descendants
D) Lapitas's descendants

22

Which of the following choices provides the best transition in the final sentence?

A) NO CHANGE
B) However, when Europeans arrived in the Pacific
C) Although when the Europeans arrived in the Pacific
D) Though Europeans arrived in the Pacific

CONTINUE

Questions 23-33 are based on the following passage.

Epic

George Eliot was one of the most prominent writers of the Victorian era. She was born Mary Ann Evans but used a male pen name because, according to her, she wanted to keep her work from being associated with the light-hearted romance novels written by many **23** women at the time. Although she followed acclaimed British female novelist **24** antecedents like Jane Austen and the Bronte sisters, she made her way in a literary field dominated by men.

[1] Eliot's novel *Middlemarch* is widely considered a modern epic—a text in the line of Homer's *Odyssey*, Virgil's *Aeneid,* and Dante's *Inferno.* [2] *Inferno* is followed by *Purgatorio* and *Paradiso.* [3] At close to eight hundred pages, *Middlemarch* depicts the interwoven lives of an entire community with intricate nuance and immense scope. [4] The modern epic is not about crashing battles or dealings with gods; instead, it handles the inner lives of individuals, ordinary but meaningful. **25**

23

A) NO CHANGE

B) women at that particular time.

C) women who were writing at the time.

D) at the time.

24

A) NO CHANGE

B) forebears

C) ancestors

D) predecessors

25

That writer plans to delete a sentence in this paragraph in order to improve its focus. Which sentence should be deleted in order to improve the focus of this paragraph?

A) Sentence 1

B) Sentence 2

C) Sentence 3

D) Sentence 4

CONTINUE

One of the central characters in *Middlemarch*, Dorothea, ardently longs to fulfill her potential in a society that does not allow women opportunities to expend their energy in [26] stimulating; challenging; meaningful ways. Furthermore, part of the novel's project is to question the possibility of the existence of heroes of either gender in the modern [27] age? She writes of the "unhistoric acts" that make up the lives of so many people in the nineteenth century, lives without "a constant unfolding of far-resonant action."

Eliot is basically right—in the modern age, there is less room for heroism. For the most part, people do not set out on adventures, [28] creating new religious orders, or embark on journeys, like the Ancient Greeks or Romans, or people in the Middle Ages. With no satisfying outlet for their ardor, people end up living [29] unextraordinarily, and if they make the world better they do so only through their "unhistoric acts."

26

A) NO CHANGE

B) stimulating, challenging, and meaningful

C) stimulating, challenging, meaningful, and

D) stimulating—challenging, meaningful

27

A) NO CHANGE

B) age…

C) age;

D) age.

28

A) NO CHANGE

B) do not create

C) create

D) are not creating

29

The writer would like to divide this sentence into two sentences at the underlined portion. Which choice most effectively accomplishes this goal?

A) unextraordinarily, and they make the world better. So, only

B) unextraordinarily, and they make the world better. They do so only

C) unextraordinarily. If they make the world better, they do so only

D) unextraordinarily, and they make the world better if they do so. Only

CONTINUE

30 Although in *Middlemarch* Eliot demonstrates how difficult it is to do great things, particularly for women at that time, she herself made something exceptional and enduring. Thus, despite how extraordinarily successful her piece is at relaying her questions and meaning, her very act of writing the book complicates its premise. She, a woman and an individual in the modern age, exerted herself to create something **31** epic in scale and lasting in impact. Her means of doing so reflects the changing state of the world: the age of warriors and adventurers is past, so her historic act is writing a book. Her "far-resonant" act is of a **32** quieter more domestic kind, but it is still a triumph. **33**

30

A) NO CHANGE
B) However, in
C) Because in
D) In conclusion, in

31

A) NO CHANGE
B) eternal and of the highest order.
C) better than the average novel.
D) subversive and objectionable to the modest Victorians.

32

A) NO CHANGE
B) quieter, more
C) quieter: more
D) quieter—more

33

The writer is considering inserting the following phrase at the end of the final sentence:

"achieved a few decades after the height of the Industrial Revolution."

Should the phrase be inserted?

A) Yes, because it provides the historical context which is necessary to understand Eliot's accomplishment.
B) Yes, because it serves as a reminder of the triumphs of Eliot's contemporaries.
C) No, because it does not relate to the significance of Eliot's work.
D) No, because the historical nature of the Industrial Revolution conflicts with the passage's theme of "unhistoric acts."

CONTINUE

Questions 34-44 are based on the following passage.

The Work of a Mechanical Engineer

If you enjoy critical thinking, practical science, and **34** solving technical problems, **35** they may be interested in becoming a mechanical engineer. Possessing an inherent curiosity about how things work and using strong math and science skills, mechanical engineers develop the technology for devices that many people use daily and take for granted.

[1] Mechanical engineers study and refine their skills for years. [2] A bachelor's degree is required, as well as additional licensure in numerous states. [3] Many mechanical engineers go on to pursue master's or doctoral degrees in their specific areas of interest. [4] Along with studying physics, electricity, thermodynamics, design, and manufacturing, mechanical engineering students must develop the problem-solving skills necessary to invent new devices, or adapt existing devices to meet new goals. [5] Mechanical engineers must be able to work well in teams. [6] The trial and error necessary for the work requires patience and attention to detail. [7] This is because a group environment is frequently essential for complex projects, which demand the combined efforts of a team of engineers. [8] Mechanical engineering programs help students develop **36** competence in these particular skill sets. **37**

34

A) NO CHANGE
B) technically problem-solving
C) technical problem-solving
D) problem-solving technically

35

A) NO CHANGE
B) one
C) we
D) you

36

A) NO CHANGE
B) them.
C) these skills.
D) skills, attributes, and abilities.

37

To make this paragraph most logical, sentence [7] should be placed

 A) where it is now.
 B) before sentence 2.
 C) after sentence 4.
 D) after sentence 5.

CONTINUE

Compared to the work of some other professions, **38** the profession of mechanical engineering is often more **39** tangible; the day-to-day work of many mechanical engineers involves hands-on experimentation and fabrication. The projects that mechanical engineers work on **40** varies enormously, from designing airplanes and spaceships to developing prosthetic limbs and medical implants.

A) NO CHANGE

B) mechanical engineers are

C) the work of mechanical engineers is

D) the hands-on nature of the work is

39

A) NO CHANGE

B) genuine

C) actual

D) certain

A) NO CHANGE

B) vary

C) varied

D) varying

CONTINUE

41 Medical implants replace missing components of the body or support damaged ones. Mechanical engineers can specialize their skill sets in order to work on projects that excite them personally, from 3D printers to smartphones, and from wind turbines to robots. However, plenty of mechanical engineers also work outside of product development, using their training in fields such as consulting, administration, and defense. **42** Most recent graduates find employment in manufacturing, but many other fields are open to them and they can apply their skills in a variety of settings as their professional interests develop over time.

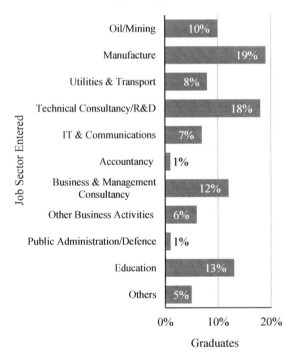

Employment Sectors of Recent Mechanical Engineering Graduates

41

The writer is considering deleting the underlined sentence. Should the sentence be deleted or kept?

A) Kept, because the example provided helps to develop the idea that mechanical engineers' work is socially important.

B) Kept, because it provides valuable additional information about the day-to-day work of mechanical engineers.

C) Deleted, because additional information about medical implants is unnecessary and distracting.

D) Deleted, because it does not contain enough specific details about the relationship between medical implants and other products.

42

Which of the following completes the sentence with the most accurate information based on the graphic?

A) NO CHANGE

B) The majority of recent graduates find jobs in manufacturing,

C) Recent graduates most often enter the field of manufacturing,

D) Less than 20% of recent graduates will find employment in relevant fields,

CONTINUE

[43] The field anticipates growth and the creation of thousands of new jobs, making it a practical choice for career-minded students. Average salaries for mechanical engineers also exceed the national average, and are rising faster than average.

However, mechanical engineering isn't merely a practical choice for those considering their job prospects: it's an opportunity to change the way people live. The work of mechanical engineers is everywhere in our society, from cars to power tools to computers. Everybody feels the effects of new technological devices without necessarily understanding how much ingenuity and skill goes into creating [44] it. We have mechanical engineers to thank for much of the technology that makes our world work.

43

Which choice most effectively establishes the main topic of the paragraph?

A) Mechanical engineers play a valuable role in society.

B) Mechanical engineers should think carefully about their job prospects before committing to this career path.

C) In our changing world, engineers will be at the forefront of the development of alternative fuels.

D) The career outlook for mechanical engineers is promising.

44

A) NO CHANGE

B) either

C) them

D) that

STOP

If you complete this section before the end of your allotted time, check your work on this section only. Do NOT use the time to work on another section.

Section 3

Math Test – No Calculator

25 MINUTES, 17 QUESTIONS

Turn to Section 3 of your answer sheet to answer the questions in this section.

DIRECTIONS

Questions **1-13** ask you to solve a problem, select the best answer among four choices, and fill in the corresponding circle on your answer sheet. Questions **14-17** ask you to solve a problem and enter your answer in a grid provided on your answer sheet. There are detailed instructions on entering answers into the grid before question 14. You may use your test booklet for scratch work.

NOTES

1. You **may not** use a calculator.
2. Variables and expressions represent real numbers unless stated otherwise.
3. Figures are drawn to scale unless stated otherwise.
4. Figures lie in a plane unless stated otherwise.
5. The domain of a function f is defined as the set of all real numbers x for which $f(x)$ is also a real number, unless stated otherwise.

REFERENCE

$A = \frac{1}{2} bh$

$a^2 + b^2 = c^2$

Special Triangles

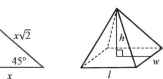

$V = \frac{1}{3} lwh$

$V = \frac{1}{3} \pi r^2 h$

$A = lw$

$V = lwh$

$V = \pi r^2 h$

$A = \pi r^2$

$C = 2\pi r$

$V = \frac{4}{3} \pi r^3$

There are 360° in a circle.

The sum of the angles in a triangle is 180°.

The number of radians of arc in a circle is 2π.

CONTINUE

1

If $x + 6 > 2x + 4$, which of the following is NOT a possible value for x?

A) -2

B) -1

C) 0

D) 2

2

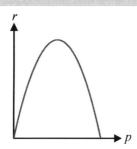

The graph above represents the revenue that a company would make from selling a product, r, as a function of the product's price, p. Which of the following equations could represent the relationship between r and p?

A) $r = p + 1900$

B) $r = -p + 1900$

C) $r = (p - 100)^2 + 2000$

D) $r = -(p - 100)^2 + 2000$

3

$$-2, 1, 4, 7\ldots$$

What is the next value in the sequence above?

A) 9

B) 10

C) 11

D) 12

4

$$y = x - 3$$
$$2x + 4y = 12$$

If (a, b) is the point of intersection of the two equations above, which of the following is correct?

A) $a \geq b$

B) $a > b$

C) $a = b$

D) $a < b$

CONTINUE

5

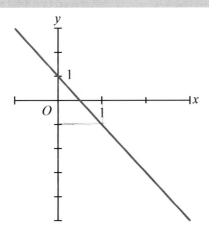

If the graph above is represented by the function $f(x) = mx + b$, what is the value of $\dfrac{m}{b}$?

A) -2

B) -1

C) 1

D) 2

6

Which of the following equations is equal to $5x^2 - 5y^2$?

    I. $5(x + y)(x - y)$

   II. $5(x + y)^2$

  III. $5(x - y)^2$

A) I only

B) I and III

C) II and III

D) I, II, and III

7

For how many ordered pairs of positive integers (x, y) is $2x + y < 5$?

A) Two

B) Four

C) Five

D) Seven

8

$$\frac{-15}{x} = \frac{11 + x}{2}$$

What is a possible value for x in the equation above?

    I.   0

   II. -5

  III. -6

  IV. -11

A) I

B) II and III

C) I and IV

D) I, II, III and IV

CONTINUE

9

What is the product of the values of y in the equation $\sqrt{3y-8} = y - 2$?

A)   6

B)   8

C)   12

D)   14

10

A research study is developing a computer program, where a pair of numbers (x, y) is rejected if their sum is greater than the absolute value of their difference. Which of the following points would be rejected by the program?

A) $(-1, -1)$

B) $(-1, 2)$

C) $(-2, 3)$

D) $(1, 1)$

11

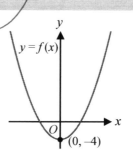 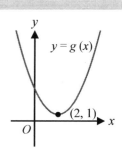

The figures above show the graphs of the functions f and g. The function f is defined by $f(x) = x^2 - 4$. The function g is defined by $g(x) = f(x - h) + k$, where h and k are constants. What is the value of hk?

A)   1

B)   2

C)   5

D)   10

CONTINUE

12

$$y = 7x + 8$$
$$y = 2x^2 + 3x + 2$$

The equations of a line and a parabola are shown above. The line and the parabola intersect at one point in the first quadrant. What are the coordinates of that point?

A) $(2, 22)$

B) $(3, 29)$

C) $(4, 36)$

D) $(5, 43)$

13

Bedrooms Available Per Household	
Number of Bedrooms	Number of Houses Available
2	5
3	15
4	29
5	47

A developer wants to estimate neighborhood population. Household size is estimated by the number of bedrooms, b, in a house, h. A summary of the neighborhood's available houses is shown on the chart above. Which of the following equations could represent the relation between b and h?

A) $h = b + 3$

B) $h = 3b - 1$

C) $h = b^2 + 1$

D) $h = 2b^2 - 3$

CONTINUE

DIRECTIONS

Questions **14-17** ask you to solve a problem and enter your answer in the grid provided on your answer sheet. When completing grid-in questions:

1. You are required to bubble in the circles for your answers. It is recommended, but not required, that you also write your answer in the boxes above the columns of circles. Points will be awarded based only on whether the circles are filled in correctly.

2. Fill in only one circle in a column.

3. You can start your answer in any column as long as you can fit in the whole answer.

4. For questions 14-17, no answers will be negative numbers.

5. **Mixed Numbers,** such as $4\frac{2}{5}$, must be gridded as decimals or improper fractions, such as 4.4 or as 22/5. "42/5" will be read as "forty-two over five," not as "four and two-fifths."

6. If your answer is a **decimal** with more digits than will fit on the grid, you may round it or cut it off, but you must fill the entire grid.

7. If there are **multiple correct solutions** to a problem, all of them will be considered correct. Enter only **one** on the grid.

CONTINUE

14

The function f is defined by $f(x) = 2 - x$. If $2f(p) = 8$, what is $f(2p)$?

15

If $-x + 2 \geq 3k$ and $x \leq 1$, what is the smallest possible value for k?

16

$$-\frac{3}{x+1} = \frac{x-10}{2x}$$

What positive value of x satisfies the equation above?

17

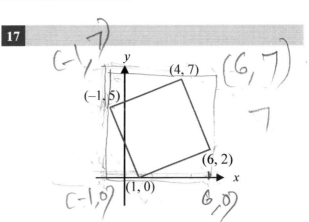
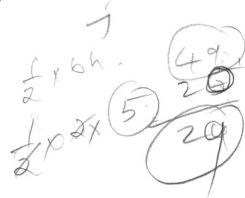

What is the area of the square in the diagram above?

STOP

If you complete this section before the end of your allotted time, check your work on this section only. Do NOT use the time to work on another section.

Section 4

Math Test – Calculator

45 MINUTES, 31 QUESTIONS

Turn to Section 4 of your answer sheet to answer the questions in this section.

DIRECTIONS

Questions **1-27** ask you to solve a problem, select the best answer among four choices, and fill in the corresponding circle on your answer sheet. Questions **28-31** ask you to solve a problem and enter your answer in a grid provided on your answer sheet. There are detailed instructions on entering answers into the grid before question 28. You may use your test booklet for scratch work.

NOTES

1. You **may** use a calculator.
2. Variables and expressions represent real numbers unless stated otherwise.
3. Figures are drawn to scale unless stated otherwise.
4. Figures lie in a plane unless stated otherwise.
5. The domain of a function f is defined as the set of all real numbers x for which $f(x)$ is also a real number, unless stated otherwise.

REFERENCE

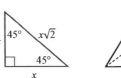

$A = \frac{1}{2} bh$ $\qquad$ $a^2 + b^2 = c^2$ $\qquad$ Special Triangles $\qquad$ $V = \frac{1}{3} lwh$ $\qquad$ $V = \frac{1}{3} \pi r^2 h$

$A = lw$ $\qquad$ $V = lwh$ $\qquad$ $V = \pi r^2 h$ $\qquad$ $A = \pi r^2$ $\qquad$ $V = \frac{4}{3}\pi r^3$

$C = 2\pi r$

There are 360° in a circle.

The sum of the angles in a triangle is 180°.

The number of radians of arc in a circle is 2π.

CONTINUE

1

If $2(-3x + c) = \dfrac{-3(2c^2 + cx)}{c} + 5c$, what is the value of x in terms of c?

A) $-\dfrac{c}{2}$

B) $\dfrac{c}{2}$

C) c

D) $2c$

2

The mean of a set of 6 integers is 30. When one of the numbers is removed, the new mean is 34. What was the number that was removed?

A) Four

B) Five

C) Eight

D) Ten

3

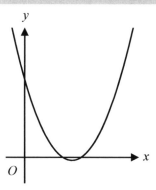

The function $y = x^2 - 5x + 6$ is graphed in the figure above. What is the y-intercept?

A) 2

B) 3

C) 5

D) 6

4

A linear function $f(x)$ passes through the origin $(0, 0)$ and the point $(3, 1)$. What is the value of $f(x)$ when $x = 6$?

A) 2

B) 3

C) 6

D) 9

CONTINUE

5

$$\frac{x}{2} + 3 \leq 2x - 9$$

In the above inequality, which of the following is NOT a possible value for x?

A) 12

B) 9

C) 8

D) 6

6

Which of the following scenarios represent(s) linear growth?

   I. A company hires 10 new employees every other year.
   II. A population of rodents increases by 10% every month.
   III. A child grows 3 inches every year.

A) I only

B) I and II only

C) I and III only

D) II and III only

Questions 7 and 8 refer to the following information.

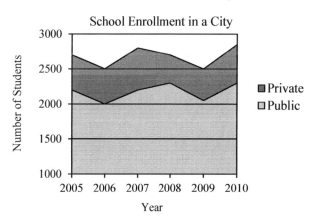

7

The graph above shows enrollment for school in a city during the years 2005 to 2010. How many total students were enrolled in 2009?

A) 2000

B) 2500

C) 2750

D) 3000

8

From 2007 to 2008, the total number of students decreased due to which of the following?

   I. A decrease in students in the public sector.
   II. A decrease in student in the private sector.

A) I

B) II

C) I and II

D) None of the above.

CONTINUE

9

Zoologists are studying finches in the Borneo forest and are looking to estimate the number and kind of finches that they will see. In the specific area that they are investigating in the forest, there are twice as many spotted finches as black finches, and half as many gray finches as black finches. If a finch is captured at random for observation, what is the probability that it will be a spotted finch?

A) $\dfrac{1}{7}$

B) $\dfrac{2}{7}$

C) $\dfrac{3}{7}$

D) $\dfrac{4}{7}$

10

x	2	3	4	5
$f(x)$	7	9	11	13

The table above gives values of the function f for selected values of x. Which of the following defines $f(x)$?

A) $f(x) = -x + 9$

B) $f(x) = x + 5$

C) $f(x) = 2x + 3$

D) $f(x) = 3x + 1$

11

If $x^2 + x = 20$, which of the following is true?

A) $x^2 - x < 10$

B) $10 < x^2 - x < 12$

C) $11 < x^2 - x < 31$

D) $31 < x^2 - x$

12

Events occur at a rate of a per week. If the number of events decreases by 25%, how many events will occur over the course of the next 28 days, in terms of a?

A) a

B) $a \times 0.75$

C) $a \times 3$

D) $a \times 4$

CONTINUE

13

Stock Prices of Companies

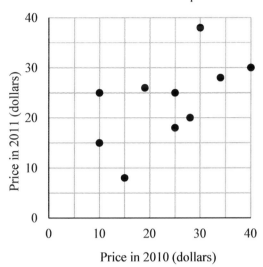

According to the graph above, how many companies saw an increase in stock price from 2010 to 2011?

A) 4

B) 5

C) 6

D) 7

14

On a test, each correct answer is worth 2 points and each incorrect answer or unanswered question reduces the score by 1 point. If the test has 45 questions and a final score of 45 is calculated, how many questions are answered correctly?

A) 15

B) 30

C) 40

D) 45

15

Container C can hold 70 milliliters of fluid. If the container is filled and dumped on the ground at a rate of 60 times per minute, how much fluid will fall to the ground in 5 minutes?

A) 18L

B) 20L

C) 21L

D) 24L

16

If $x + y = 9$ and $x^2 + y^2 = 45$, what are possible values for x?

A) $x = 6, x = 3$

B) $6 > x > 3$

C) $x = 6, x = -3$

D) $3 > x \geq -6$

CONTINUE

17

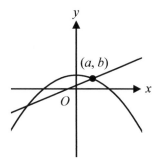

The functions $y = -x^2 + 4$ and $y = 2x + 1$ are graphed above. What is the value of ab?

A) -9

B) -3

C) 3

D) 15

18

The sum of two integers is twice their difference. If one of the integers is 6, which of the following is a NOT a possible value for the other integer?

A) 2

B) 12

C) 18

D) The value cannot be determined.

19

Rules for a Card Game	
Card Type	Number of Points
Odd	Multiply number on card by 2
Even	Multiply number on card by 3

In a card game, Jenny draws three cards from a deck of ten unique cards labeled 1 through 10. The number of points for each card is calculated using the rules listed above and added together for the total score. If Jenny has a total score of 48, and two of her cards are 3 and 6, which of the following must have been her third card?

A) 2

B) 4

C) 6

D) 8

20

A random integer is selected from 1000 different integers from 1 to 1000. What is the probability that the integer is divisible by both 3 and 5?

A) $\dfrac{3}{50}$

B) $\dfrac{13}{200}$

C) $\dfrac{33}{500}$

D) $\dfrac{67}{1000}$

CONTINUE

21

Stock Prices of Three Companies		
	2010	2011
Company A	$50.25	$51.75
Company B	$35.80	$37.80
Company C	$46.90	$49.40

The table above shows the stock prices for three companies during the years 2010 and 2011. Which company had the greatest percent increase in stock prices from 2010 to 2011?

A) Company A

B) Company B

C) Company C

D) Companies B and C shared the highest increase in stock prices.

22

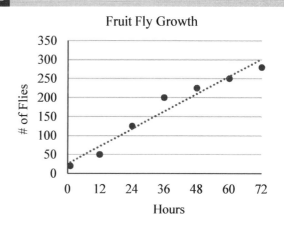

Fruit Fly Growth

The fruit fly, *Drosophila melanogaster*, has an astonishing rate of reproduction. In a controlled experiment, biologists introduce 20 flies into a habitat. They chart the number of flies in the area every 12 hours, as shown above. Which of the following is NOT correct?

A) The rate that flies are being born fluctuates as time progresses.

B) The period of largest growth occurred between 36 and 48 hours.

C) Based on the line of best fit, a good prediction for the number of flies at 84 hours is 350.

D) The number of flies grew quickly for the first half of the experiment and then grew less quickly as time progressed.

CONTINUE

23

System of Integers and Their Values	
Number of Integers	Value per Integer
1	$3d$
3	e
6	f

There are five groups of numbers. Three of these groups contain single integers, one group contains three integers, and one group contains six integers. The mean value of each size of group is shown in the table above. What is the mean value of the integers in all of the groups?

A) $d + e + 2f$

B) $3d + 3e + 6f$

C) $9d + 3e + 6f$

D) $\dfrac{3d + e + 2f}{4}$

24

Event v occurs 28% of the time on Tuesdays, and event v and event w occur together 19% of the time on Tuesdays. Given that event v occurs on a Tuesday, what is the probability that event w occurs with event v?

A) 47%

B) 58%

C) 68%

D) 75%

25

$$g(2x + 1) = 4g(x) + x + 1$$
$$g(1) = 3$$

Two values for $g(x)$ are defined above. What is the value of $g(3)$?

A) 10

B) 14

C) 18

D) 22

26

The average of a set of four numbers is x. When a fifth number is added to the set, the average of the numbers is $x + 2$. In terms of x, what is the number that was added?

A) $x + 2$

B) $x + 5$

C) $x + 8$

D) $x + 10$

27

$$y = -(x + 2)^2 + 9$$

The parabola with the equation shown above has x-intercepts of $(a, 0)$ and $(b, 0)$. What is $|a + b|$?

A) 2

B) 4

C) 5

D) 6

CONTINUE

DIRECTIONS

Questions **28-31** ask you to solve a problem and enter your answer in the grid provided on your answer sheet. When completing grid-in questions:

1. You are required to bubble in the circles for your answers. It is recommended, but not required, that you also write your answer in the boxes above the columns of circles. Points will be awarded based only on whether the circles are filled in correctly.

2. Fill in only one circle in a column.

3. You can start your answer in any column as long as you can fit in the whole answer.

4. For questions 28-31, no answers will be negative numbers.

5. **Mixed Numbers,** such as $4\frac{2}{5}$, must be gridded as decimals or improper fractions, such as 4.4 or as 22/5. "42/5" will be read as "forty-two over five," not as "four and two-fifths."

6. If your answer is a **decimal** with more digits than will fit on the grid, you may round it or cut it off, but you must fill the entire grid.

7. If there are **multiple correct solutions** to a problem, all of them will be considered correct. Enter only **one** on the grid.

CONTINUE

28

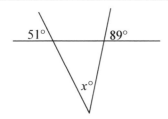

What is the value of x in the figure above?

29

Points $(-1, 2)$ and $(2, 11)$ lie on the line s. If p is perpendicular to s, and $(0, 5)$ lies on p, what is the y-coordinate of the point where s and p intersect?

Questions 30 and 31 refer to the following information.

The volume of the oceans on Earth is approximately 1,386 million km^3. As the Earth's temperature rises, the ice in the polar icecaps melts into the oceans, increasing the volume of the oceans. If 1 cm^3 of ice melts, it turns into approximately 0.92 cm^3 water.

30

There are approximately 3,800 cm^3 in a gallon. If 1.9 m^3 of ice melts, how many gallons of water does this produce? (Round your answer to the nearest gallon.)

31

Scientists estimate that the addition of 1,000 km^3 of water would increase sea levels by 364 cm. Greenland's ice sheet is especially vulnerable to melting. Recent reports indicate a melting average of 195 km^3 of ice per year from Greenland, resulting in additional yearly 179.4 km^3 of water. If melting continues at this rate, how many centimeters would the sea level increase after six years? (Round your answer to the nearest centimeter.)

STOP

If you complete this section before the end of your allotted time, check your work on this section only. Do NOT use the time to work on another section.

PRACTICE TEST 2

PSAT

Directions

- Work on just one section at a time.
- If you complete a section before the end of your allotted time, use the extra minutes to check your work on that section only. Do NOT use the time to work on another section.

Using Your Test Booklet

- No credit will be given for anything written in the test booklet. You may use the text booklet for scratch paper.
- You are not allowed to continue answering questions in a section after the allotted time has run out. This includes marking answers on your answer sheet that you previously noted in your test booklet.
- You are not allowed to fold pages, take pages out of the test booklet, or take any pages home.

Answering Questions

- Each answer must be marked in the corresponding row on the answer sheet.
- Each bubble must be filled in completely and darkly within the lines.

  Correct ●   Incorrect

- Be careful to bubble in the correct part of the answer sheet.
- Extra marks on your answer sheet may be marked as incorrect answers and lower your score.
- Make sure you use a No. 2 pencil.

Scoring

- You will receive one point for each correct answer.
- Incorrect answers will NOT result in points deducted. Even if you are unsure about an answer, you should make a guess.

**DO NOT BEGIN THIS TEST
UNTIL YOUR PROCTOR TELLS YOU TO DO SO**

Download printable answer sheets, answer keys, and Excel scoring sheets from:

ivyglobal.com/study

SECTION 1

1 Ⓐ Ⓑ Ⓒ Ⓓ	11 Ⓐ Ⓑ Ⓒ Ⓓ	21 Ⓐ Ⓑ Ⓒ Ⓓ	31 Ⓐ Ⓑ Ⓒ Ⓓ	41 Ⓐ Ⓑ Ⓒ Ⓓ
2 Ⓐ Ⓑ Ⓒ Ⓓ	12 Ⓐ Ⓑ Ⓒ Ⓓ	22 Ⓐ Ⓑ Ⓒ Ⓓ	32 Ⓐ Ⓑ Ⓒ Ⓓ	42 Ⓐ Ⓑ Ⓒ Ⓓ
3 Ⓐ Ⓑ Ⓒ Ⓓ	13 Ⓐ Ⓑ Ⓒ Ⓓ	23 Ⓐ Ⓑ Ⓒ Ⓓ	33 Ⓐ Ⓑ Ⓒ Ⓓ	43 Ⓐ Ⓑ Ⓒ Ⓓ
4 Ⓐ Ⓑ Ⓒ Ⓓ	14 Ⓐ Ⓑ Ⓒ Ⓓ	24 Ⓐ Ⓑ Ⓒ Ⓓ	34 Ⓐ Ⓑ Ⓒ Ⓓ	44 Ⓐ Ⓑ Ⓒ Ⓓ
5 Ⓐ Ⓑ Ⓒ Ⓓ	15 Ⓐ Ⓑ Ⓒ Ⓓ	25 Ⓐ Ⓑ Ⓒ Ⓓ	35 Ⓐ Ⓑ Ⓒ Ⓓ	45 Ⓐ Ⓑ Ⓒ Ⓓ
6 Ⓐ Ⓑ Ⓒ Ⓓ	16 Ⓐ Ⓑ Ⓒ Ⓓ	26 Ⓐ Ⓑ Ⓒ Ⓓ	36 Ⓐ Ⓑ Ⓒ Ⓓ	46 Ⓐ Ⓑ Ⓒ Ⓓ
7 Ⓐ Ⓑ Ⓒ Ⓓ	17 Ⓐ Ⓑ Ⓒ Ⓓ	27 Ⓐ Ⓑ Ⓒ Ⓓ	37 Ⓐ Ⓑ Ⓒ Ⓓ	47 Ⓐ Ⓑ Ⓒ Ⓓ
8 Ⓐ Ⓑ Ⓒ Ⓓ	18 Ⓐ Ⓑ Ⓒ Ⓓ	28 Ⓐ Ⓑ Ⓒ Ⓓ	38 Ⓐ Ⓑ Ⓒ Ⓓ	
9 Ⓐ Ⓑ Ⓒ Ⓓ	19 Ⓐ Ⓑ Ⓒ Ⓓ	29 Ⓐ Ⓑ Ⓒ Ⓓ	39 Ⓐ Ⓑ Ⓒ Ⓓ	
10 Ⓐ Ⓑ Ⓒ Ⓓ	20 Ⓐ Ⓑ Ⓒ Ⓓ	30 Ⓐ Ⓑ Ⓒ Ⓓ	40 Ⓐ Ⓑ Ⓒ Ⓓ	

SECTION 2

1 Ⓐ Ⓑ Ⓒ Ⓓ	11 Ⓐ Ⓑ Ⓒ Ⓓ	21 Ⓐ Ⓑ Ⓒ Ⓓ	31 Ⓐ Ⓑ Ⓒ Ⓓ	41 Ⓐ Ⓑ Ⓒ Ⓓ
2 Ⓐ Ⓑ Ⓒ Ⓓ	12 Ⓐ Ⓑ Ⓒ Ⓓ	22 Ⓐ Ⓑ Ⓒ Ⓓ	32 Ⓐ Ⓑ Ⓒ Ⓓ	42 Ⓐ Ⓑ Ⓒ Ⓓ
3 Ⓐ Ⓑ Ⓒ Ⓓ	13 Ⓐ Ⓑ Ⓒ Ⓓ	23 Ⓐ Ⓑ Ⓒ Ⓓ	33 Ⓐ Ⓑ Ⓒ Ⓓ	43 Ⓐ Ⓑ Ⓒ Ⓓ
4 Ⓐ Ⓑ Ⓒ Ⓓ	14 Ⓐ Ⓑ Ⓒ Ⓓ	24 Ⓐ Ⓑ Ⓒ Ⓓ	34 Ⓐ Ⓑ Ⓒ Ⓓ	44 Ⓐ Ⓑ Ⓒ Ⓓ
5 Ⓐ Ⓑ Ⓒ Ⓓ	15 Ⓐ Ⓑ Ⓒ Ⓓ	25 Ⓐ Ⓑ Ⓒ Ⓓ	35 Ⓐ Ⓑ Ⓒ Ⓓ	
6 Ⓐ Ⓑ Ⓒ Ⓓ	16 Ⓐ Ⓑ Ⓒ Ⓓ	26 Ⓐ Ⓑ Ⓒ Ⓓ	36 Ⓐ Ⓑ Ⓒ Ⓓ	
7 Ⓐ Ⓑ Ⓒ Ⓓ	17 Ⓐ Ⓑ Ⓒ Ⓓ	27 Ⓐ Ⓑ Ⓒ Ⓓ	37 Ⓐ Ⓑ Ⓒ Ⓓ	
8 Ⓐ Ⓑ Ⓒ Ⓓ	18 Ⓐ Ⓑ Ⓒ Ⓓ	28 Ⓐ Ⓑ Ⓒ Ⓓ	38 Ⓐ Ⓑ Ⓒ Ⓓ	
9 Ⓐ Ⓑ Ⓒ Ⓓ	19 Ⓐ Ⓑ Ⓒ Ⓓ	29 Ⓐ Ⓑ Ⓒ Ⓓ	39 Ⓐ Ⓑ Ⓒ Ⓓ	
10 Ⓐ Ⓑ Ⓒ Ⓓ	20 Ⓐ Ⓑ Ⓒ Ⓓ	30 Ⓐ Ⓑ Ⓒ Ⓓ	40 Ⓐ Ⓑ Ⓒ Ⓓ	

SECTION 3

1 Ⓐ Ⓑ Ⓒ Ⓓ	11 Ⓐ Ⓑ Ⓒ Ⓓ
2 Ⓐ Ⓑ Ⓒ Ⓓ	12 Ⓐ Ⓑ Ⓒ Ⓓ
3 Ⓐ Ⓑ Ⓒ Ⓓ	13 Ⓐ Ⓑ Ⓒ Ⓓ
4 Ⓐ Ⓑ Ⓒ Ⓓ	
5 Ⓐ Ⓑ Ⓒ Ⓓ	
6 Ⓐ Ⓑ Ⓒ Ⓓ	
7 Ⓐ Ⓑ Ⓒ Ⓓ	
8 Ⓐ Ⓑ Ⓒ Ⓓ	
9 Ⓐ Ⓑ Ⓒ Ⓓ	
10 Ⓐ Ⓑ Ⓒ Ⓓ	

Grid-in questions 14, 15, 16, 17

1 Ⓐ Ⓑ Ⓒ Ⓓ
2 Ⓐ Ⓑ Ⓒ Ⓓ
3 Ⓐ Ⓑ Ⓒ Ⓓ
4 Ⓐ Ⓑ Ⓒ Ⓓ
5 Ⓐ Ⓑ Ⓒ Ⓓ
6 Ⓐ Ⓑ Ⓒ Ⓓ
7 Ⓐ Ⓑ Ⓒ Ⓓ
8 Ⓐ Ⓑ Ⓒ Ⓓ
9 Ⓐ Ⓑ Ⓒ Ⓓ
10 Ⓐ Ⓑ Ⓒ Ⓓ

11 Ⓐ Ⓑ Ⓒ Ⓓ
12 Ⓐ Ⓑ Ⓒ Ⓓ
13 Ⓐ Ⓑ Ⓒ Ⓓ
14 Ⓐ Ⓑ Ⓒ Ⓓ
15 Ⓐ Ⓑ Ⓒ Ⓓ
16 Ⓐ Ⓑ Ⓒ Ⓓ
17 Ⓐ Ⓑ Ⓒ Ⓓ
18 Ⓐ Ⓑ Ⓒ Ⓓ
19 Ⓐ Ⓑ Ⓒ Ⓓ
20 Ⓐ Ⓑ Ⓒ Ⓓ

21 Ⓐ Ⓑ Ⓒ Ⓓ
22 Ⓐ Ⓑ Ⓒ Ⓓ
23 Ⓐ Ⓑ Ⓒ Ⓓ
24 Ⓐ Ⓑ Ⓒ Ⓓ
25 Ⓐ Ⓑ Ⓒ Ⓓ
26 Ⓐ Ⓑ Ⓒ Ⓓ
27 Ⓐ Ⓑ Ⓒ Ⓓ

28 / grid
29 / grid
30 / grid
31 / grid

Section 1

Reading Test

60 MINUTES, 47 QUESTIONS

Turn to Section 1 of your answer sheet to answer the questions in this section.

DIRECTIONS

Every passage or paired set of passages is accompanied by a number of questions. Read the passage or paired set of passages, then use what is said or implied in what you read and in any given graphics to choose the best answer to each question.

Questions 1-9 are based on the following passage.

This passage is adapted from a speech delivered by President William Jefferson Clinton. The speech was given to Congress as his State of the Union Address in 1998.

Because of the hard work and high purpose of the American people, these are good times for America. We have more than 14 million new jobs,
Line the lowest unemployment in 24 years, the lowest
5 core inflation in 30 years. Incomes are rising, and we have the highest homeownership in history. Crime has dropped for a record five years in a row and the welfare rolls are at their lowest level in 27 years. Our leadership in the world is unrivaled.
10 Ladies and gentlemen, the state of our union is strong.

But with barely 700 days left in the 20th Century, this is not a time to rest; it is a time to build, to build the America within our reach.
15 An America where everybody has a chance to get ahead with hard work. Where families are strong, schools are good, and all our young people can go on to college. An America where every child can stretch a hand across a keyboard and reach
20 every book ever written, every painting ever painted, every symphony ever composed. An America which leads the world to new heights of peace and prosperity.

This is the America we have begun to build; this
25 is the America we can leave to our children if we join together to finish the work at hand.

Rarely have Americans lived through so much change, in so many ways, in so short a time. Quietly but with gathering force, the ground has shifted
30 beneath our feet, as we have moved into an Information Age, a global economy, a truly new world. The Information Age is first and foremost an education age in which education must start at birth and continue throughout a lifetime.
35 Last year from this podium I said that education has to be our highest priority. I laid out a ten-point plan to move us forward and urged all of us to let politics stop at the schoolhouse door. Since then, this Congress, across party lines, and the American
40 people have responded in the most important year for education in a generation, expanding public school choice, opening the way to 3,000 new charter schools, working to connect every classroom in the country to the information superhighway,
45 committing to expand Head Start to a million children, launching America Reads, sending literally thousands of college students into our elementary schools to make sure all our 8-year-olds can read.

Last year I proposed and you passed 220,000
50 new Pell Grant scholarships for deserving students. Student loans are already less expensive and easier to repay. Now you get to deduct the interest.

CONTINUE

Families all over America now can put their
savings into new tax-free education IRAs. And
55   this year for the first 2 years of college families
will get a $1,500 tax credit, a Hope Scholarship
that will cover the cost of most community
college tuition.

And because of these actions, I have
60   something to say to every family listening to us
tonight: your children can go on to college.
Because of the things that have been done, we can
make college as universal in the 21st century as
high school is today. And, my friends, that will
65   change the face and future of America.

We have opened wide the doors of the world's
best system of higher education. Now we must
make our public elementary and secondary
schools the world's best as well by raising
70   standards, raising expectations, and raising
accountability.

1

Clinton's tone is best described as

A) serene.

B) anxious.

C) optimistic.

D) arrogant.

2

Clinton supports the assertion that the country is
thriving by

A) listing sections of his previous ten-point
development plan that have finally been
realized.

B) listing facts and figures that compare the
present with other times in the nation's
history.

C) sharing a personal anecdote of how his own
life has improved within the past year.

D) appealing to his listeners' emotions by
discussing the impressive history of the nation.

3

Which choice provides the best evidence for the
answer to the previous question?

A) Lines 7-9 ("Crime has … years")

B) Lines 12-14 ("But with … reach")

C) Lines 24-26 ("This is … hand")

D) Lines 53-54 ("Families all … IRAs")

CONTINUE

4

In lines 19-21, why does Clinton describe an America where every child can "reach every book ever written, every painting ever painted, every symphony ever composed"?

A) He wants to emphasize the importance of the humanities, and not just the sciences, in the new education system.

B) He is concerned about falling literacy rates among the youngest members of the population and hopes computers can help.

C) He fears changes in the Information Age will make students less likely to seek out cultural knowledge and experiences.

D) He is looking forward to a time when children will have unprecedented access to information to further their education.

5

As used in line 29, "force" most nearly means

A) violence.

B) influence.

C) momentum.

D) dynamism.

6

According to the passage, which of the following best expresses the relationship between education and the Information Age?

A) Education and the Information Age will grow in tandem.

B) Education is a necessary prerequisite for the Information Age.

C) Education and the Information Age are mutually exclusive.

D) Breakthroughs in education have led to the Information Age.

7

Which choice provides the best evidence for the answer to the previous question?

A) Lines 32-34 ("The Information … lifetime")

B) Lines 49-50 ("Last year … students")

C) Lines 62-64 ("Because of … today")

D) Lines 67-71 ("Now we … accountability")

8

In the passage, Clinton's use of the phrase "let politics stop at the schoolhouse door" (lines 37-38) is meant to convey the idea that

A) while Congress should legislate on access to education, they should refrain from legislating on curricula.

B) politicians should refrain from visiting schools during election season to avoid improper influence.

C) Congress should pay attention to education when coming up with an agenda for the year.

D) members of Congress should not let political differences prevent them from working together on education reform.

9

According to the passage, one reason college will be within reach for many students is because

A) student loans have been universally forgiven by the Pell Grants.

B) new Hope Scholarships will cover the entire cost of a college education.

C) interest on student loans is at an all-time low.

D) a new type of IRA will help families save for college.

CONTINUE

Questions 10-19 are based on the following passage.

This passage is adapted from Elizabeth Bernstein, "How You Make Decisions Says a Lot About How Happy You Are." ©2014 by *Dow Jones & Company*.

Psychology researchers have studied how people make decisions and concluded there are two basic styles. "Maximizers" like to take their time and
Line weigh a wide range of options—sometimes every
5 possible one—before choosing. "Satisficers" would rather be fast than thorough; they prefer to quickly choose the option that fills the minimum criteria (the word "satisfice" blends "satisfy" and "suffice"). "Maximizers are people who want the very best.
10 Satisficers are people who want good enough," says Barry Schwartz, a professor of psychology at Swarthmore College in Pennsylvania.

In a study published in 2006 in the journal Psychological Science, Dr. Schwartz and colleagues
15 followed 548 job-seeking college seniors at 11 schools from October through their graduation in June. Across the board, they found that the maximizers landed better jobs. Their starting salaries were, on average, 20% higher than those of the
20 satisficers, but they felt worse about their jobs. "The maximizer is kicking himself because he can't examine every option and at some point had to just pick something," Dr. Schwartz says. "Maximizers make good decisions and end up feeling bad about
25 them. Satisficers make good decisions and end up feeling good." Dr. Schwartz says he found nothing to suggest that either maximizers or satisficers make bad decisions more often.

Satisficers also have high standards, but they are
30 happier than maximizers, he says. Maximizers tend to be more depressed and to report a lower satisfaction with life, his research found. The older you are, the less likely you are to be a maximizer— which helps explain why studies show people get
35 happier as they get older.

Dr. Schwartz says he found men are no more or less likely than women to be either satisficers or

maximizers. He hasn't researched whether people tend to pair up with mates who have similar, or
40 opposite, decision-making styles—or how they make decisions with a partner. People with opposite styles might be better off together because they balance each other out, he theorizes. Standards will be high, but decisions will get made. "If you are
45 both maximizers, neither of you will be able to relinquish your standards," Dr. Schwartz says.

David Gerzof Richard makes quick, decisive choices. His wife, Brooke, likes to research every option. The spouses say they didn't learn to make
50 decisions together until after an event early in their marriage that they refer to as "the car."

Mr. Richard decided the couple needed a new car to replace their old one. He spent a few days researching SUVs, found a good deal on an Audi Q5
55 and signed the lease—without telling his wife. Ms. Richard wasn't happy when he told her. At her insistence, the spouses spent the weekend test-driving five more cars. The couple stuck with the Q5—Ms. Richard agreed that it remained the best
60 deal—but they both learned something about how their decision-making styles could complement each other's. "His decision-making makes it so we can get it done faster and don't lose opportunities," Ms. Richard says. "And my decision-making makes sure
65 we are truly not forgetting to consider what is important."

In most cases, whoever cares most about the result should choose, Dr. Schwartz says. This isn't the same as always letting the maximizer decide. If
70 the maximizer is paralyzed with indecision, it can work best if the satisficer chooses, Dr. Schwartz says. Many mismatched couples find it helps to let the person with the higher standards decide—lest the satisficer pick something that isn't up to the
75 maximizer's standards. Either way, couples should talk about the decision and narrow down the possibilities together.

CONTINUE

Reactions to Increasing Choice

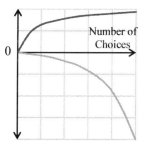

10

Which of the following best describes the structure of the passage as a whole?

A) The author defines two personality traits, elaborates on the differences between them, and uses an example to show how they can create both conflict and harmony.

B) The author states a thesis, discounts much of that thesis using statistics, then ultimately disagrees with that thesis.

C) The author defines different ways that people make decisions and explains that these decisions can lead to a happier marriage.

D) The author uses personal examples to describe how people with different decision-making personalities can come to agreement.

11

According to the passage, on average younger people are more likely than older people to

A) seek relationships with a satisficer.

B) take their time weighing all options.

C) be satisficers themselves.

D) make bad decisions.

12

It can be reasonably inferred from the passage that

A) a couple consisting of two satisficers will make decisions quickly.

B) a couple consisting of two satisficers will never fight.

C) a couple consisting of two maximizers will make better decisions than a couple consisting of two satisficers.

D) a couple consisting of two satisficers will be unhappier than a couple consisting of two maximizers.

13

Which choice provides the best evidence for the answer to the previous question?

A) Lines 5-8 ("'Satisficers would' … suffice")

B) Lines 29-30 ("Satisficers also … says")

C) Lines 38-41 ("He hasn't … partner")

D) Lines 72-75 ("Many mismatched … standards")

14

Which of the following is most analogous to the author's description of a maximizer in lines 3-5 ("'Maximizers' like … choosing")?

A) A couple wishing to buy a home visits two houses in a neighborhood in one morning and chooses one that afternoon.

B) A man buys two different ties because he can wear them both to different events.

C) A student studies a wide range of math problems to prepare for her calculus test.

D) A teenager visits a sporting goods store multiple times over a few months to test different baseballs before making a purchase.

CONTINUE

15

As used in line 4, "weigh" most nearly means

A) measure.

B) assay.

C) count.

D) consider.

16

Which best summarizes the story of Mr. and Ms. Richards?

A) A maximizer and satisficer will have many arguments in their marital life.

B) Although it can be hard, a maximizer and satisficer can learn to make decisions together.

C) A maximizer may feel compelled to accept his or her spouse's rash decisions.

D) While they might disagree at first, maximizers and satisficers always agree in the end.

17

Which choice provides the best evidence for the answer to the previous question?

A) Lines 44-46 ("If you ... says")

B) Lines 49-51 ("The spouses ... car")

C) Lines 58-62 ("The couple ... other's")

D) Lines 69-72 ("If the ... says")

18

As used in line 70, "paralyzed" most nearly means

A) shocked.

B) rendered immobile.

C) overwhelmed.

D) dazed.

19

Based on the graphic and passage, which of the following could be a reason why satisficers tend to be happier than maximizers?

A) Increasing choice creates more good feelings as well as more bad feelings, and maximizers make more choices.

B) Increasing choice creates more bad feelings than good feelings, and satisficers consider fewer options.

C) Increasing choice creates more bad feelings than good feelings, and satisficers avoid making choices.

D) Increasing choice creates more good feelings than bad feelings, and satisficers are able to make more choices than maximizers.

CONTINUE ▶

Questions 20-28 are based on the following passage.

This passage is adapted from Pam Belluck, "To Improve a Memory, Consider Chocolate." ©2014 by *The New York Times Company*.

Science recently edged closer to showing that an antioxidant in chocolate appears to improve some memory skills that people lose with age. In a small
Line study healthy people, ages 50 to 69, who drank a
5 mixture high in antioxidants called cocoa flavanols for three months performed better on a memory test than people who drank a low-flavanol mixture.

On average, the improvement of high-flavanol drinkers meant they performed like people two to
10 three decades younger on the study's memory task, said Dr. Scott A. Small, a neurologist at Columbia University Medical Center and the study's senior author. They performed about 25 percent better than the low-flavanol group. The findings support recent
15 research linking flavanols, especially epicatechin, to improved blood circulation, heart health and memory in mice, snails and humans. But experts said the new study, although involving only 37 participants and partly funded by Mars Inc., the
20 chocolate company, goes further and was a well-controlled, randomized trial led by experienced researchers.

Besides improvements on the memory test—a pattern recognition test involving the kind of skill
25 used in remembering where you parked the car or recalling the face of someone you just met—researchers found increased function in an area of the brain's hippocampus called the dentate gyrus, which has been linked to this type of memory. "This
30 is really interesting to see it in three months," said Dr. Steven DeKosky, a neurologist and visiting professor at the University of Pittsburgh. "They got this really remarkable increase in a place in the brain that we know is related to age-related memory
35 change." There was no increased activity in another region, the entorhinal cortex, which is impaired early in Alzheimer's disease. That reinforces the idea that age-related memory decline is different and suggests

that flavanols might not help Alzheimer's, even
40 though they might delay normal memory loss.

But unless you are stocking up for Halloween, do not rush to buy Milky Way or Snickers bars. To consume the high-flavanol group's daily dose of epicatechin, 138 milligrams, would take eating at
45 least 300 grams of dark chocolate a day—about seven average-sized bars. Or possibly about 100 grams of baking chocolate or unsweetened cocoa powder, but concentrations vary widely depending on the processing. Milk chocolate has most
50 epicatechin processed out of it. "You would have to eat a large amount of chocolate," along with its fat and calories, said Hagen Schroeter, director of fundamental health and nutrition research for Mars, which funds many flavanol studies and approached
55 Dr. Small for this one. "I nearly threw them out," said Dr. Small, who added that he later concluded that the company employed serious scientists who would not bias the research. "Candy bars don't even have a lot of chocolate in them," Dr. Schroeter said.
60 And "most chocolate uses a process called dutching and alkalization. That's like poison for flavanol."

Mars already sells a supplement, CocoaVia, which it says promotes healthy circulation, including for the heart and brain. It contains 20 to 25
65 milligrams of epicatechin per serving, Dr. Schroeter said. Epicatechin is also in foods like tea and apples, although may be less absorbable.

The Columbia study had important limitations. For example, the only daily dietary requirements
70 were either 900 milligrams of flavanols with 138 milligrams of epicatechin or 10 milligrams of flavanols with less than two milligrams of epicatechin, so participants could have eaten other things that played a role. And while researchers also
75 had half of the healthy but sedentary participants in each group exercise four days a week, surprisingly, the exercise had no effects on memory. Dr. Small, whose research previously found that exercise helped hippocampal function in younger people,
80 suggested maybe more vigorous exercise is needed to affect older brains.

CONTINUE

More extensive research is planned. As for why flavanols would help memory, one theory is that they improve brain blood flow. Another, favored by Dr. Small, is that they cause dendrites, message-receiving branches of neurons, to grow.

85

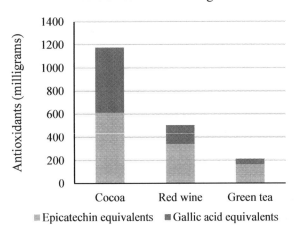

Antioxidants in Beverages

■ Epicatechin equivalents   ■ Gallic acid equivalents

20

The main point of the passage is that

A) a new study provides evidence that ingesting large amounts of an antioxidant found in chocolate can delay age-related memory loss.

B) experts agree that a new study that links cocoa flavanols to improved memory is somewhat flawed.

C) drinking large amounts of an antioxidant found in chocolate can improve memory loss in people of any age.

D) Mars, Inc. is one of several chocolate companies trying to spur research into chocolate's positive effects.

21

Which of the following, according to the passage, is the least efficient way to get the dose of epicatechin shown to improve memory in test subjects?

A) Eating dark chocolate

B) Eating baking chocolate or unsweetened cocoa powder

C) Eating milk chocolate

D) Drinking the high-antioxidant mixture from the study

22

Which choice provides the best evidence for the answer to the previous question?

A) Lines 41-42 ("But unless … bars")

B) Lines 42-46 ("To consume … bars")

C) Lines 49-50 ("Milk chocolate … it")

D) Lines 58-59 ("Candy bars … said")

23

In the passage, Dr. Small implies that he

A) was initially skeptical that the Mars Inc. study would be unbiased.

B) was overwhelmed at work and initially considered not taking on a new project.

C) originally held negative opinions about antioxidants before this study.

D) does not believe that Mars Inc. is a reputable company.

CONTINUE

24

Which choice provides evidence for the answer to the previous question?

A) Lines 8-13 ("On average … author")

B) Lines 55-58 ("I nearly … research")

C) Lines 77-81 ("Dr. Small … brains")

D) Lines 84-86 ("Another, favored … to grow")

25

Which provides the best summary of the researchers' findings?

A) High-flavonol drinkers had improved memory test results and increased function of the dentate gyrus.

B) High-flavonol drinkers had improved memory test results in spite of decreased function in the dentate gyrus.

C) High-flavonol drinkers had increased function in the dentate gyrus and increased blood flow.

D) High-flavonol drinkers had improved memory test results and increased function in the dentate gyrus and entorhinal cortex.

26

As used in line 63, "promotes" most nearly means

A) advertises.

B) encourages.

C) raises.

D) stimulates.

27

As used in line 80, "vigorous" most nearly means

A) sturdy.

B) intense.

C) vibrant.

D) vital.

28

It can be inferred from the passage and graphic that

A) while cocoa has more antioxidants and higher concentrations of epicatechin than chocolate bars, it does not have as many antioxidants as green tea and red wine.

B) while scientists have been focusing on the health benefits of epicatechin in a variety of foods, they should begin shifting to a focus on gallic acid as it may provide even greater health benefits.

C) although cocoa has more epicatechin than red wine and green tea, it would not be conducive to good health to use it as an exclusive source of antioxidants.

D) cocoa, green tea, and red wine all contain almost identical proportions of epicatechin and gallic acid, meaning green tea and red wine provide equal flavonoid benefits to cocoa.

CONTINUE

Questions 29-38 are based on the following passage.

Passage 1 is adapted from Christine Gorman, "FDA Was Right to Block 23andMe." ©2013 by *Scientific American*. Passage 2 is adapted from Katherine Harmon, "Genome Sequencing for the Rest of Us." ©2010 by *Scientific American*.

Passage 1

A few techno-libertarians are up in arms over the FDA's letter warning the genetics company 23andMe to stop selling its personalized genome
Line services kit. But a quick search shows federal
5 regulators have been targeting various low-cost genetic testing ventures to provide the necessary analysis that goes along with a proper genetic screening for at least the past three years.

At present, getting raw data about your personal
10 genome is worse than useless, as Nancy Shute pointed out in a Scientific American article that I edited back in 2012. "[E]ach individual's genetic readout must be compared with lots and lots of other people's readouts for doctors to understand which
15 genetic patterns are important indicators of disease and which can be safely ignored," she wrote.

Shute further quoted Euan A. Ashley, an assistant professor of cardiology at the Stanford University School of Medicine as saying, "'Generating the
20 sequence now is fast and cheap. . . But the analysis? Wow. That's not going to be fast, and that's not going to be cheap.'"

Using home gene kits to imagine where your ancestors might hail from is one thing. That's
25 basically the 21st century equivalent of looking up your horoscope—entertaining but not really a matter of life and death. Cheap sequence data from 23andMe and other gene testing companies has much greater potential to harm without the proper
30 interpretation of the results. Unfortunately, this is still quite difficult and expensive in most cases.

Passage 2

In the quest to better know one's self, more and more people are turning to genome sequencing to uncover information about their ancestral histories,
35 impending health risks, and disorders of potential progeny. Despite the completion of the generalized human genome draft a decade ago, connections between diseases and genetic variations have proved to be complex and elusive.

40 Some conditions, such as cystic fibrosis (pinpointed even before the completion of the human genome), are caused by single gene mutations, and clinical genetic tests for these types of diseases have been useful diagnostic tools. But
45 other diseases, such as Alzheimer's, have no uniform genetic signature leaving many to wonder about the science and utility behind the results many genome scans offer casual consumers.

Even for genetic tests that offer just a snapshot of
50 relatively common disease-linked variations, the amount of data such a scan generates is immense and requires distillation before relevant information can be presented to consumers. This process of interpretation, however, is one place where the
55 science can get murky.

Most companies offer genetic data in terms of relative risk for particular conditions. Some provide links to scientific studies about genetic variants that appear in your genome, allowing a customer to
60 judge what a particular difference might mean for them.

That approach could have limitations for much of the public who might not be interested in sifting through a decade of scientific literature about a
65 particular mutation they carry.

Another challenge to consumer genetic testing has been consistency. Although most sequencing processes are similar, and the DNA itself is a unique code, reports from various groups for a single person
70 can have striking differences. "People interpret the information that comes out of the sequence differently," notes John Boyce, co-founder of Delphi Bio, a biotech consulting firm.

CONTINUE

The main problem, as explained by Boyce and
75 others, is that solid, predictive biomarkers have
not been agreed on for most conditions. "The
sample populations are not large enough to truly
find the predictive biomarkers," Boyce says.

Another company Boyce is involved with,
80 GnuBio, aims to drop the cost of sequencing to
$30 per genome in the next two years. With fast
and cheap sequencing, he expects the number of
logged genomes will skyrocket. "Once the
numbers [of genomes] are high enough," Boyce
85 says, "we should… find the predictive
biomarkers."

29

The main point of Passage 1 is that

A) obtaining raw data about one's personal
genome is likely prohibitively costly and could
be incorrect.

B) home genome sequencing kits are unhelpful
and could have serious drawbacks.

C) the medical community agrees that the costs of
genome testing currently far outweigh the
benefits.

D) the FDA has been actively trying to come up
with more cost-effective ways to test genetic
sequences.

30

Which choice provides the best evidence for the
answer to the previous question?

A) Lines 4-8 ("But a … years")

B) Lines 9-12 ("At present … 2012")

C) Lines 24-27 ("That's basically … death")

D) Lines 27-30 ("Cheap sequence … results")

31

The tone of the author of Passage 1 is best
described as

A) horrified.

B) frustrated.

C) academic.

D) critical.

32

As used in line 30, the word "interpretation" most
closely means

A) understanding.

B) exposition.

C) portrayal.

D) rendition.

33

As used in line 52, "distillation" most nearly
means

A) cleansing.

B) purification.

C) clarification.

D) condensation.

CONTINUE

34

Which of the following would provide the best evidence in support of the argument in lines 74-78 of Passage 2 ("The main … says")?

A) Scientists have reached some consensus regarding most predictive biomarkers.

B) Special computer programs can easily hypothesize expected predictive biomarkers from a small sample size.

C) Predictive biomarkers could be assembled from years of currently assembled genomes.

D) Finding predictive biomarkers is a surprisingly expensive endeavor.

35

Which best describes the relationship between the two passages?

A) Both passages recognize the current limitations of genome sequencing, but Passage 2 is more hopeful about its potential benefits.

B) Neither Passage 1 nor Passage 2 discusses any benefits to personalized genome sequencing.

C) Passage 2 notes some of the common problems with home genome sequencing that Passage 1 discusses in depth.

D) Passage 1 appears to have been written as a response to Passage 2.

36

All of the following are mentioned in either Passage 1, Passage 2, or both as potential benefits of genome sequences EXCEPT

A) researching where family ancestors are from.

B) looking for genetic indicators of disease.

C) determining what health risks descendants may be prone to.

D) extending the average life span.

37

In response to Shute's critique of genome sequencing in lines 12-22 of Passage 1, the author of Passage 2 would likely argue that

A) companies are working to reduce the cost of sequencing, which will simultaneously allow more genomes to be logged.

B) there are actually more predictive biomarkers than Shute acknowledges and the difficulty lies in interpreting the data with these markers.

C) most diseases, like cystic fibrosis, can be readily determined without comparing one's genome to others'.

D) Shute has overemphasized the importance of comparing one's genetic sequence to others'.

38

Which choice provides the best evidence for the answer to the previous question?

A) Lines 40-44 ("Some conditions … tools")

B) Lines 57-61 ("Some provide … them")

C) Lines 70-73 ("People … firm")

D) Lines 81-83 ("With fast … skyrocket")

CONTINUE

Questions 39-47 are based on the following passage.

This passage is adapted from Robert Louis Stevenson, *"Story of the House with the Green Blinds,"* originally published in 1878.

Francis Scrymgeour, a clerk in the Bank of Scotland at Edinburgh, had attained the age of twenty-five in a sphere of quiet, creditable, and
Line domestic life. Francis, who was of a docile and
5 affectionate disposition, devoted himself heart and soul to his employment. He grew rapidly in favor with his superiors, and enjoyed already a salary of nearly two hundred pounds a year, with the prospect of an ultimate advance to almost double that amount.
10 One day he received a note from a well-known firm of Writers to the Signet, requesting an immediate interview with him. The letter was marked "Private and Confidential," and had been addressed to him at the bank, instead of at home—
15 two unusual circumstances which made him obey the summons with more alacrity. The senior member of the firm made him gravely welcome, requested him to take a seat, and proceeded to explain the matter in hand in the picked expressions of a veteran
20 man of business. A person, who must remain nameless, but of whom the lawyer had every reason to think well, desired to make Francis an annual allowance of five hundred pounds. There were conditions annexed to this liberality, but he was of
25 opinion that his new client would find nothing either excessive or dishonorable in the terms; and he repeated these two words with emphasis, as though he desired to commit himself to nothing more.
Francis asked their nature. "The conditions," said
30 the Writer to the Signet, "are, as I have twice remarked, neither dishonorable nor excessive. At the same time I cannot conceal from you that they are most unusual. Indeed, the whole case is very much out of our way; and I should certainly have refused it
35 had it not been for the reputation of the gentleman who entrusted it to my care."

Francis entreated him to be more specific. "They are two," replied the lawyer, "only two; and the sum, as you will remember, is five hundred a year."
40 And the lawyer raised his eyebrows at him with solemn gusto. "The first," he resumed, "is of remarkable simplicity. You must be in Paris by the afternoon of Sunday, the 15th; there you will find, at the box-office of the Comedie Francaise, a ticket for
45 admission taken in your name and waiting you. You are requested to sit out the whole performance in the seat provided, and that is all."
"The other is of more importance," continued the Writer to the Signet. "It regards your marriage. My
50 client, taking a deep interest in your welfare, desires to advise you absolutely in the choice of a wife. Absolutely, you understand," he repeated.
"Sir," said Francis, "after a piece of news so startling, you must grant me some hours for thought.
55 You shall know this evening what conclusion I have reached."
The lawyer commended his prudence; and Francis, excusing himself upon some pretext at the bank, took a long walk into the country. He fully
60 considered the different steps and aspects of the case. His whole carnal man leaned irresistibly towards the five hundred a year, and the strange conditions with which it was burdened; he began to despise the narrow and unromantic interests of his
65 former life. When once his mind was fairly made up, he walked with a new feeling of strength and freedom.

CONTINUE

39

In the beginning of the passage, Francis is portrayed as

A) a man who works hard and has been rewarded for his efforts.

B) a scholar who enjoys the finer things in life.

C) an orphan who has achieved success at a young age.

D) a clerk who dislikes his job but makes a lot of money.

40

The passage most strongly suggests that Francis finds the offer

A) attractive because he has been struggling financially despite his dedication to his work.

B) tempting because of both its large sum and the excitement of the conditions attached to it.

C) unambiguously appealing given the conditions and amount.

D) upsetting due to the fact that he will lose control over choosing his own spouse.

41

Which choice provides the best evidence for the answer to the previous question?

A) Lines 6-9 ("He grew … amount")

B) Lines 31-33 ("At the … unusual")

C) Lines 53-54 ("Sir, said … thought")

D) Lines 61-65 ("His whole … life")

42

As used in line 9, "ultimate" most nearly means

A) eventual.

B) fundamental.

C) elemental.

D) quintessential.

43

The Writer clearly finds the deal he is offering Francis to be

A) incredibly exciting, but unusual.

B) of solemn importance, but markedly simple.

C) commendable in size but questionable given its origin.

D) strange, but still worth considering given its source.

44

Which choice provides the best evidence for the answer to the previous question?

A) Lines 12-16 ("The letter … alacrity")

B) Lines 33-36 ("Indeed, the … care")

C) Lines 37-39 ("They are … year")

D) Lines 41-42 ("The first … simplicity")

45

As used in line 17, "gravely" most nearly means

A) badly.

B) concernedly.

C) menacingly.

D) solemnly.

CONTINUE

46

Which of the following is the reason the lawyer commends Francis on his "prudence" (line 57)?

A) Francis decides not to take the offer.

B) Francis asks for some time to think over the offer.

C) Francis's employer speaks highly of him.

D) Francis does not care what the conditions of the offer are.

47

Francis most likely "walked with a new feeling of strength and freedom" (line 66-67) because he had decided

A) to take the offer and was excited about the choice he had made.

B) to take the offer and was nervous about what would come next.

C) not to take the offer and was relieved to be done with the matter.

D) not to take the offer and was second-guessing that decision.

STOP

If you complete this section before the end of your allotted time, check your work on this section only. Do NOT use the time to work on another section.

Section 2

Writing and Language Test

35 MINUTES, 44 QUESTIONS

Turn to Section 2 of your answer sheet to answer the questions in this section.

DIRECTIONS

Every passage comes with a set of questions. Some questions will ask you to consider how the writer might revise the passage to improve the expression of ideas. Other questions will ask you to consider correcting potential errors in sentence structure, usage, or punctuation. There may be one or more graphics that you will need to consult as you revise and edit the passage.

Some questions will refer to a portion of the passage that has been underlined. Other questions will refer to a particular spot in a passage or ask that you consider the passage in full.

After you read the passage, select the answers to questions that most effectively improve the passage's writing quality or that adjust the passage to follow the conventions of standard written English. Many questions give you the option to select "NO CHANGE." Select that option in cases where you think the relevant part of the passage should remain as it currently is.

Questions 1-11 are based on the following passage.

Sports Accounting: A Numbers Game

Everyone knows accountants and star athletes have nothing in common; one group crunches numbers while the other group crushes the competition. These **1** professions do however overlap in the business offices of the professional sports industry, where accountants play **2** an essential role behind the scenes, helping to make what happens on the field possible.

1

A) NO CHANGE
B) professions do, however, overlap
C) professions however do overlap
D) professions do. However, overlap

2

A) NO CHANGE
B) a fundamental
C) an imperative
D) an obligatory

CONTINUE

[1] Beyond just tracking debits and credits, sports accountants perform such tasks as analyzing costs, developing budgets, creating financial statements, and more. [2] All sports franchises have accountants who are involved in every aspect of the financial life of the team. [3] One particularly complex task in the field of sports accounting is payroll. [4] Athletic contracts can be very complex, **3** with: incentives for high performance; bonuses for meeting specific conditions; and penalties for violating codes of conduct. [5] Overseeing the compensation of athletes can be a challenging task, but one component may be something sports accountants already love: tracking the stats of players on their favorite teams. **4**

To qualify for a job as a sports accountant, a candidate needs a minimum of a four-year degree in accounting, though an additional degree, **5** such as an MBA degree, may provide an edge. That edge can help prospective accountants to land exactly the jobs they want, but there are many opportunities in the field. Every major team **6** need accountants and so does smaller teams and many private clubs. One potential dream job for the sports-fan accountant hoping for direct contact with a star athlete would be working with a sports agent or manager.

3

A) NO CHANGE

B) with incentives for high performance bonuses for meeting specific conditions and penalties for violating codes of conduct.

C) with; incentives, for high performance, bonuses, for meeting specific conditions, and penalties, for violating codes of conduct.

D) with incentives for high performance, bonuses for meeting specific conditions, and penalties for violating codes of conduct.

4

To make this paragraph most logical, sentence 2 should be placed

A) where it is now.

B) after sentence 3.

C) before sentence 1.

D) after sentence 4.

5

A) NO CHANGE

B) such as an MBA

C) an MBA is an advantage

D) candidates with an MBA

6

A) NO CHANGE

B) need accountants, and so do

C) needs an accountant, and so does

D) needs an accountant, and so do

CONTINUE

Accountants in general tend to be well-compensated, so accounting is a practical choice for those who consider good compensation to be a high priority. Accountants in the spectator sports industry tend to accept slightly lower salaries on average than **7** their counterparts; in other corporate environments, **8** whereas it is still a very sensible choice. The Bureau of Labor Statistics reported that the average salary for all accountants was $68,000 in 2011, while that of sports accountants in particular was $70,000.

9 Anyone who gets to work in this field is in a fortunate position. The perks include tickets to games and the chance to rub elbows with elite athletes. Best of all, perhaps, **10** was that sports accounting provided an opportunity for sports fans to be a part of their favorite teams. For some people, that makes sports accounting an **11** acceptable profession.

7

A) NO CHANGE

B) their counterparts, in

C) their counterparts in

D) their counterparts in,

8

A) NO CHANGE

B) but

C) because

D) as

9

A) NO CHANGE

B) Beyond financial rewards, there are also other benefits to working as a sports accountant.

C) How much an accountant gets paid depends, to a large degree, on where they work.

D) Nearly every profession also has certain non-financial benefits.

10

A) NO CHANGE

B) is that sports accounting provides

C) was that sports accounting provides

D) is that sports accounting provided

11

A) NO CHANGE

B) awesome way to make a living

C) amazing gig

D) excellent career choice

CONTINUE

Questions 12-22 are based on the following passage:

King Philip's War

In late January of 1675, a Native American who had taken the name John Sassamon disappeared. Sassamon, just weeks before, [12] he had met with the leader of the governor of the Plymouth Colony, Josiah Winslow. The purpose of this meeting was to warn Winslow that the Wampanoag chief Metacom (whom the English called "King Philip") was hoping to join forces with other Native American leaders to drive the English settlers out of New England. Winslow sent Sassamon away, certain that the warning was some kind of trick. Shortly after his disappearance, Sassamon's body was found submerged in an [13] icy pond based on the condition of his corpse, it was determined that he had been murdered. Within months, three Native American men were accused of, convicted of, and executed [14] by Sassamon's murder. Within weeks of the executions of the alleged murderers, King Philip's War began.

12

A) NO CHANGE
B) had met
C) he met
D) met

13

A) NO CHANGE
B) icy pond. Based on
C) icy pond and based on
D) icy pond, based on

14

A) NO CHANGE
B) of
C) through
D) for

CONTINUE

Known also as Metacom's Rebellion, this conflict was the last in a series of efforts by the Native Americans to rid New England of the colonists. [15] The Wampanoags themselves had actually been among the first Native Americans to befriend the members of the Plymouth Colony. [16] Shockingly, Philip was the son of Massasoit, the leader who had greeted the Mayflower pilgrims. Massasoit was probably responsible for helping teach the pilgrims to plant corn, which was essential to their survival, and it is said that he was the one who invited the Pilgrims to the First Thanksgiving.

15

Which choice, inserted here, results in the most effective transition to the information that follows in the paragraph?

A) Metacom, or Metacomet, was a Native American leader, but before the conflict he had appeared in Plymouth to request an English name, and received the name "Philip."

B) The reasons for conflicts are always complex, but Metacom's Rebellion was an exception.

C) Thus, Sassamon's murder was not merely an isolated tragedy; rather, it was the catalyst for a whole cascade of tragic outcomes.

D) However, the Native Americans involved in the conflict had not always been opposed to English presence.

16

A) NO CHANGE

B) It's unbelievable that Philip

C) Even more surprising, Philip

D) In fact, Philip

CONTINUE

What, then, were the causes of King Philip's War? Some historians claim the conflict was [17] inevitable; it was a clash of cultures that simply could not have been avoided. [18] The English and Native Americans had never lived so closely, and tensions were high. Others place the blame on features of the Pilgrims' culture. They believed that the New World had been divinely promised to them, and expanded their settlements rapidly. There is no single cause agreed upon by historians. [19] In light of these facts, this war was probably the bloodiest of all these so-called uprisings.

17

A) NO CHANGE

B) predicted

C) interminable

D) preordained

18

The writer is considering deleting the underlined sentence. Should the underlined sentence be kept or deleted?

A) Kept, because it helps to establish the timeline of important events leading up to the war

B) Kept, because it provides support for the claim that the war resulted from a clash of cultures

C) Deleted, because it doesn't provide support for the alleged causes of the war

D) Deleted, because it blurs the paragraph's focus on the reasons for tensions between the English settlers and the Native Americans

19

A) NO CHANGE

B) Whatever its causes,

C) In spite of these factors,

D) In conclusion,

CONTINUE

Over the course of the fourteen-month war, twelve towns were destroyed and around 5,000 people had **20** died, approximately three-quarters of them, were Native Americans. The devastation faced by Native Americans **21** were not confined to death, though. Some survivors escaped to Canada, uprooted and displaced, while others were captured. 180 of those survivors were sent to the Caribbean on a ship named the Seaflower. **22**

20

A) NO CHANGE

B) died, approximately three-quarters were Native Americans.

C) died approximately three-quarters of them were Native Americans.

D) died, approximately three-quarters of whom were Native Americans.

21

A) NO CHANGE

B) have not been

C) are not

D) was not

22

The writer wants to conclude the passage with a sentence that somberly emphasizes the tragic fate of the Native Americans on the Seaflower. Which choice would best accomplish this goal?

A) This ship, with a name so similar to the Mayflower that brought the Pilgrims to freedom, now carried the descendants of Massosoit and other Native Americans to slavery.

B) The name of the ship echoes that of the Pilgrim's Mayflower, but the Seaflower is far less well-known and served a very different purpose.

C) Those survivors weren't going down to the islands for a Caribbean vacation, they were being sent as slaves!

D) In summary, while the causes of the war may remain a mystery, its outcomes are all too clear: the bloody conflict left many dead on both sides, and many others in slavery.

CONTINUE

Questions 23-33 are based on the following passage:

"Show And Tell"

"Show, don't tell." This is the singular imperative in writers' workshops, in articles about 23 writing, in Composition 101. There is wisdom in that rule. 24 By showing rather than telling, a writer creates a more accessible story for her readers. Readers want to have access to the scene into which they are being invited; 25 we want to get involved in the action and to feel as if they can almost touch the characters and the scenery. However, "showing" or, more accurately, narrative, does only half the job of the writer involved in memoir or personal essay. 26 Without insight born of exposition, no matter how evocative the narrative, the result is simply "words on paper."

23

A) NO CHANGE
B) writing, and in
C) writing; and in
D) writing, and; in

24

A) NO CHANGE
B) By showing rather than telling, a more accessible story is created by the writer for her readers.
C) A more accessible story is created by the writer for her readers, showing rather than telling.
D) By showing rather than telling, readers can find a writer's story to be more accessible.

25

A) NO CHANGE
B) one wants
C) they want
D) she wants

26

Which sentence, inserted here, best helps to establish the main point of the paragraph?

A) To fully tell the story, the writer needs to create a rich setting.
B) If the writer only uses narrative, there will be something missing from the essay.
C) The writer has to also have a certain amount of insight into the subject.
D) That writer must "tell as well as show," by using exposition to provide the essential element of the genre: insight.

CONTINUE

One writer who succeeds at both telling and showing is the **27** notorious Joan Didion, a celebrated novelist and journalist. A specific example of her success is her essay, "In Bed." This essay explores what it is like to suffer from migraines. **28** The essay tells the story of Didion's specific experience of migraine. However, it also contains a great deal of factual exposition, explaining what migraine is (and is not), presenting a case against the perception that those who suffer from migraines are "malingerers," **29** and providing information about the treatment of the malady. The tone she uses throughout is authoritative; Didion presents herself as an expert on **30** this and her intention seems to be to educate those who are not affected by the malady. Though she is telling a personal tale, Didion seems to be examining the event of a migraine from a distance in order to express an idea directly while placing her ideas about the event outside of time.

27

A) NO CHANGE

B) renowned

C) infamous

D) acknowledged

28

Which choice would result in the most effective transition to the following sentences?

A) NO CHANGE

B) The essay provides both a personal story and information about migraines.

C) As a migraine sufferer, Didion undoubtedly has strong feelings about the topic, but manages to temper her feelings with facts.

D) The essay is an interesting and compelling piece of writing.

29

The writer wants to complete the sentence with a third example that best reflects Didion's use of exposition. Which choice most effectively accomplishes this goal?

A) NO CHANGE

B) and telling stories about how other people experience migraines.

C) and making the reader feel as though they have a personal connection with Didion.

D) and using vivid imagery to draw the reader into the story.

30

A) NO CHANGE

B) migraines

C) this point

D) that

CONTINUE

[1] "In Bed" is not merely a dry recitation of facts, though. [2] There is a great story being told, complete with all the necessary **31** parts she uses setting, characters, and specific details that bring the story alive. [3] Didion is such a master of the writing craft that, even with minimal narrative, she makes a reader feel as if they have been given a guided tour of a foreign country. [4] She also offers up a startling insight: that there is a kind of peace to be found in giving in to the magnified anxiety and pain that cannot be ignored. **32**

33 Admittedly, that is the most surprising thing of all. Through her sparing use of narrative amidst all that exposition, Joan Didion delivers a revelation about something beyond her apparent subject.

31

A) NO CHANGE
B) parts, she
C) parts, which she
D) parts. She

32

Which sentence should be deleted to improve the focus of the paragraph?

A) Sentence 1
B) Sentence 2
C) Sentence 3
D) Sentence 4

33

A) NO CHANGE
B) Furthermore,
C) Therefore,
D) Ultimately,

CONTINUE

Questions 34-44 are based on the following passage:

Masting Maples: Seeds, Syrup, and Sap

In March and April each year, just as winter releases its grip on the eastern half of the U.S. and Canada, an army equipped with spouts, hooks, buckets, and miles of plastic tubing takes to the woods. [34] Consequently, this army is not going into battle; these are sugarmakers, and their forays into the woods signal the start of sugaring season. Their goal is to capture the sap of sugar maples, the source of the most beloved topping for pancakes and [35] waffles maple syrup.

[1] Traditionally, sugarmakers have attributed sap production to weather conditions. [2] It takes approximately forty gallons of maple sap to make one gallon of syrup. [3] However, the amount of syrup each tree yields varies from one year to another depending on the amount of sap produced. [4] Extreme cold during the winter or the early advent of warm temperatures in the spring can lead to decreased sap production. [5] Yet when researchers looked at data for several years of syrup production, weather alone was not sufficient explanation for [36] fluctuations in syrup yields year-to-year. [37]

34

A) NO CHANGE
B) Therefore
C) Furthermore
D) However

35

A) NO CHANGE
B) waffles, maple syrup.
C) waffles. Maple syrup.
D) waffles: maple syrup.

36

A) NO CHANGE
B) flexes
C) instabilities
D) volatilities

37

To make this paragraph most logical, sentence 1 should be placed

A) NO CHANGE
B) after sentence 3.
C) after sentence 4.
D) after sentence 2.

CONTINUE

38 Maple trees are a *mast* species: they tend to seed in synchronized cycles, with all of the trees in a stand seeding together in the same year. Mast years **39** led to a depletion of available energy stores, and long intervals of low-seed years in which the trees replenish their stores. Those same energy stores likely determine the amount of sugar present in the sap of the **40** trees. Following a mast year, then, the amount of sugar in the sap may be lower, thus **41** affecting syrup production.

38

Which choice, inserted here, provides the most effective transition between paragraphs?

A) These fluctuations are a serious problem: sugarmakers have tight budgets, and unexpected losses can have a serious impact.

B) It's notable, however, that temperatures are the best predictor of daily sap yields.

C) Obligate seeders die back in fire or other disasters, and resprout from buried roots or dormant seeds, claiming land from nearby plants.

D) Recently, however, scientists have been exploring whether it is possible to predict the amount of syrup maple trees will produce by looking at the seed cycles of the trees.

39

A) NO CHANGE

B) leads

C) lead

D) leading

40

A) NO CHANGE

B) trees'

C) tree's

D) trees's

41

A) NO CHANGE

B) effecting

C) affected

D) effected

CONTINUE

[42] Because syrup is produced by boiling off the sap water in order to produce syrup, higher ratios of sugar in sap mean increased output of syrup. That means that information about seeding should be able to help predict syrup output. When researchers examined data on seed production and syrup yields in subsequent years, their results seemed to show that [43] more trees seeding in one year means more sap sugar in the next year.

Since the harvest lasts only about two months and requires long work days, up to 16 hours, knowing ahead of time whether it's going to be a "good syrup year" could make a world of difference to the sugarmakers. Predicting sap yields more accurately would allow sugarmakers to better forecast profits for a specific stand of trees in a specific year, making it easier for [44] one to budget more effectively.

42

A) NO CHANGE

B) Boiling off the sap water is necessary

C) In order to produce syrup, the sap water is boiled off, therefore

D) Because the sap water is boiled off

43

Which choice completes the sentence with accurate data based on the graphs?

A) NO CHANGE

B) more sap sugar in one year means more seeds in the next year.

C) more syrup in one year means less sap sugar in the next year.

D) more trees seeding in one year means less syrup in the next year.

44

A) NO CHANGE

B) they

C) them

D) whom

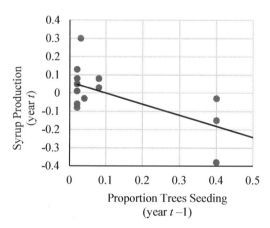

This table shows the relationship of syrup production in year *t* to seed production in the previous year, year *t* − 1.

STOP

If you complete this section before the end of your allotted time, check your work on this section only. Do NOT use the time to work on another section.

Section 3

Math Test – No Calculator

25 MINUTES, 17 QUESTIONS

Turn to Section 3 of your answer sheet to answer the questions in this section.

DIRECTIONS

Questions **1-13** ask you to solve a problem, select the best answer among four choices, and fill in the corresponding circle on your answer sheet. Questions **14-17** ask you to solve a problem and enter your answer in a grid provided on your answer sheet. There are detailed instructions on entering answers into the grid before question 14. You may use your test booklet for scratch work.

NOTES

1. You **may not** use a calculator.
2. Variables and expressions represent real numbers unless stated otherwise.
3. Figures are drawn to scale unless stated otherwise.
4. Figures lie in a plane unless stated otherwise.
5. The domain of a function f is defined as the set of all real numbers x for which $f(x)$ is also a real number, unless stated otherwise.

REFERENCE

$A = \frac{1}{2} bh$

$a^2 + b^2 = c^2$

$x\sqrt{3}$

Special Triangles

$V = \frac{1}{3} lwh$

$V = \frac{1}{3}\pi r^2 h$

$A = lw$

$V = lwh$

$V = \pi r^2 h$

$A = \pi r^2$

$C = 2\pi r$

$V = \frac{4}{3}\pi r^3$

There are 360° in a circle.

The sum of the angles in a triangle is 180°.

The number of radians of arc in a circle is 2π.

CONTINUE

1

If $3x + 5 = x + 15$, what is the value of x?

A) 1

B) 3

C) 5

D) 7

3

If $-2x + 12 = 2y$, what is the value of $x + y$?

A) 12

B) 10

C)   8

D)   6

2

x	$f(x)$
–1	–1
2	5
5	11
6	13

Which of the following equations describes the chart above?

A) $f(x) = 2x - 1$

B) $f(x) = 2x + 1$

C) $f(x) = x - 1$

D) $f(x) = x + 1$

4

If $f(x) = 10x + 2$, and $g(x) = -2(8 - 2x)$, what is the value of y at the point of their intersection?

A) –28

B) –14

C) –5

D)   0

CONTINUE

5

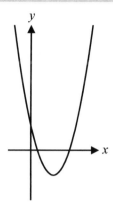

The graph above could be a representation of which of the following equations?

A) $y = (x - 3)^2 + 3$

B) $y = (x + 3)^2 + 3$

C) $y = (x - 3)^2 - 3$

D) $y = (x + 3)^2 - 3$

6

If $4y - x > 8$, and $x = 4$, what must be true about y?

A) $y > -3$

B) $y < -3$

C) $y < 3$

D) $y > 3$

7

Each of the following are equivalent to $ax + 3x^2$ EXCEPT:

A) $x(a + 3x)$

B) $\dfrac{2abx + 6bx^2}{2b}$

C) $a\left(3x + \dfrac{5x^2}{a}\right) - 2(x^2 + ax)$

D) $\dfrac{3ax + 3x^2}{3}$

8

To participate in a school field trip, a student must be at least 10 years old but no older than 14. If a is the age of the student, which of the following represents students who qualify for the trip?

A) $|a - 10| \leq 4$

B) $|10 - a| \geq 4$

C) $|a - 12| \leq 2$

D) $|14 - a| \leq 2$

CONTINUE

9

A statistician is compiling neighborhood demographics for an apartment building in New York City. She determines that there are 46 male and female residents in the building. One month after her census, 6 male residents move out of the building, resulting in 3 times as many female as male residents in the apartment building. How many female residents were originally in the building?

A) 16

B) 28

C) 30

D) 40

10

$$\frac{14x^2 - 13x - 12}{2x - 3}$$

Which of the following polynomials is equal to the fraction shown above?

A) $6x + 5$

B) $7x - 2$

C) $7x + 4$

D) $8x + 6$

11

t	$P(t)$
0	15
1	45
2	135
3	405
4	1215

The table above shows the population of a culture of amoeba grown in a laboratory that triples every hour. Which of the following equations represents $P(t)$, the population of amoeba, as a function of t, the time in hours since the beginning of the experiment?

A) $P(t) = 15(3t)$

B) $P(t) = 15(3)^t$

C) $P(t) = 15t^3$

D) $P(t) = 15(t + 1)^3$

CONTINUE

12

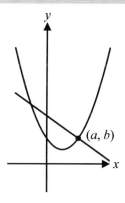

The graphs of the parabola $y = x^2 - 4x + 9$ and the line $y = -2x + 17$ are shown above. What is the value of $a + b$?

A) 10

B) 13

C) 17

D) 19

13

Which of the following expressions is equivalent to $\dfrac{6x^2 + 4x + 3xy + 2y}{3x + 2}$?

A) $x + 2y$

B) $2x + y$

C) $2x + 2y$

D) $3x + y$

CONTINUE

DIRECTIONS

Questions **14-17** ask you to solve a problem and enter your answer in the grid provided on your answer sheet. When completing grid-in questions:

1. You are required to bubble in the circles for your answers. It is recommended, but not required, that you also write your answer in the boxes above the columns of circles. Points will be awarded based only on whether the circles are filled in correctly.

2. Fill in only one circle in a column.

3. You can start your answer in any column as long as you can fit in the whole answer.

4. For questions 14-17, no answers will be negative numbers.

5. **Mixed Numbers,** such as $4\frac{2}{5}$, must be gridded as decimals or improper fractions, such as 4.4 or as 22/5. "42/5" will be read as "forty-two over five," not as "four and two-fifths."

6. If your answer is a **decimal** with more digits than will fit on the grid, you may round it or cut it off, but you must fill the entire grid.

7. If there are **multiple correct solutions** to a problem, all of them will be considered correct. Enter only **one** on the grid.

CONTINUE

14

If $(4^a)(4^b) = 16$, what is the value of $6a + 6b$?

15

The parabola with the equation $y = x^2 - 8x + 16$ has an x-intercept of $(a, 0)$. What is the value of a?

16

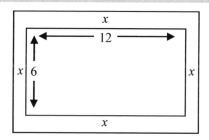

A picture measuring 6 inches by 12 inches can be placed in a frame with an area of 112 square inches. If x is the distance between the picture and the edge of the frame, what is the value of x in the figure above?

17

$$\frac{5x}{3} + y = c$$

$$2y = c - 4x$$

If $x + y = 6$, what is the value of c for the system of equations above?

STOP

If you complete this section before the end of your allotted time, check your work on this section only. Do NOT use the time to work on another section.

Section 4

Math Test – Calculator

45 MINUTES, 31 QUESTIONS

Turn to Section 4 of your answer sheet to answer the questions in this section.

DIRECTIONS

Questions **1-27** ask you to solve a problem, select the best answer among four choices, and fill in the corresponding circle on your answer sheet. Questions **28-31** ask you to solve a problem and enter your answer in a grid provided on your answer sheet. There are detailed instructions on entering answers into the grid before question 28. You may use your test booklet for scratch work.

NOTES

1. You **may** use a calculator.
2. Variables and expressions represent real numbers unless stated otherwise.
3. Figures are drawn to scale unless stated otherwise.
4. Figures lie in a plane unless stated otherwise.
5. The domain of a function f is defined as the set of all real numbers x for which $f(x)$ is also a real number, unless stated otherwise.

REFERENCE

$A = \frac{1}{2}bh$ $a^2 + b^2 = c^2$ Special Triangles $V = \frac{1}{3}lwh$ $V = \frac{1}{3}\pi r^2 h$

$A = lw$ $V = lwh$ $V = \pi r^2 h$ $A = \pi r^2$ $V = \frac{4}{3}\pi r^3$
            $C = 2\pi r$

There are 360° in a circle.

The sum of the angles in a triangle is 180°.

The number of radians of arc in a circle is 2π.

CONTINUE

1

A: 3, 7, 9, 6, 2, 3

The group of numbers A is found above. What is the median of this group of numbers?

A) 2.5

B)   3

C) 4.5

D)   5

2

A group of people consists of 18 girls and 12 boys. What fraction of the group are boys?

A) $\dfrac{2}{3}$

B) $\dfrac{3}{5}$

C) $\dfrac{2}{5}$

D) $\dfrac{1}{3}$

3

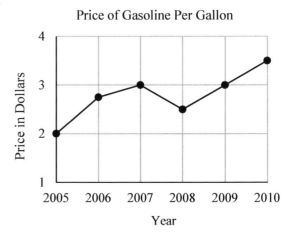

Price of Gasoline Per Gallon

The graph above shows the price of gasoline during the years 2005 to 2010. If the gas mileage for Ralph's car is 35 miles per gallon, which of the following is true?

A) It cost Ralph the same to drive 400 miles in 2005 as 200 miles in 2007.

B) It cost Ralph 15 dollars to drive 210 miles in 2008.

C) It cost Ralph more to drive per mile in 2007 than in 2009.

D) Overall, the price of gasoline is decreasing with time.

CONTINUE

4

Twice the sum of two numbers is 24. If one number is 2 times larger than the other, what is the smaller of the two numbers?

A) 2

B) 3

C) 4

D) 5

5

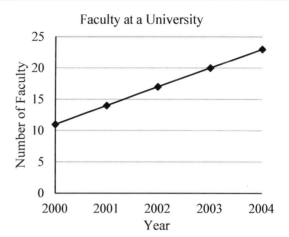

Faculty at a University

The number of faculty at a university increased linearly from 2000 to 2004, as shown in the graph above. In 2000, the economics department of a university had 11 faculty members. If the number of faculty continued to increase at the same rate, which of the following is the best estimate for the number of economics department faculty members in 2005?

A) 19

B) 20

C) 23

D) 26

CONTINUE

6

If $x = 2$ and $y = -1$, what is the difference between $1 + 2x + 5y^2$ and $4x + 3y$?

A) 2

B) 5

C) 10

D) 50

7

The sum of a group of 12 numbers is 300. If the average of two of these numbers is 40, what is the average of the remaining 10 numbers?

A) 20

B) 22

C) 26

D) 28

8

$$f(x) = 3x + 1$$
$$g(x) = x - 3$$

Using the functions above, for what value of x is $f(x) = g(x)$?

A) −4

B) −2

C) 2

D) 4

9

The yearly expenditures on office supplies at a company is linearly proportional to the number of their employees. If they spent $28,000 on 700 employees last year, how much money would they spend this year on 850 employees?

A) $30,000

B) $32,000

C) $34,000

D) $36,000

CONTINUE

Questions 10, 11, and 12 refer to the following information.

Three sets contain 90 integers. The number of integers in each set, and the number of integers shared between sets is summarized in the diagram below.

Number of Integers in Sets A, B, and C

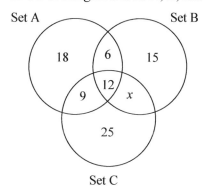

Set A   Set B

18   6   15

12

9   x

25

Set C

What is the value of x?

A)   5

B)   8

C) 10

D) 15

11

What percent of all the integers are a part of Set A?

A) 20%

B) 30%

C) 40%

D) 50%

Another set of integers, Set D, contains 50 integers. What is the ratio of integers in Set D to integers in Set A?

A)   5:9

B)   10:9

C) 25:12

D) 25:9

CONTINUE

13

Which of the following is NOT equivalent to 60% of $\frac{1}{4}$ of 320?

A) 15% of 320

B) 60% of 80

C) 25% of 192

D) 30% of 300

14

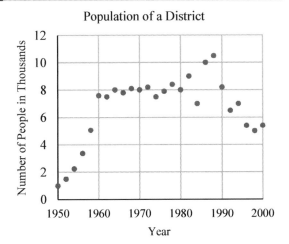

Population of a District

The scatterplot above shows the population in a city district during the years 1950 to 2000. Which of the following statements is/are supported by the plot?

    I.   The number of people grew exponentially during the years 1950 to 1960.

    II.   The population grew most quickly between 1980 and 1990.

    III.   There were approximately 8 times more people in 1960 than 1950.

A) I only

B) I and II only

C) I and III only

D) II and III only

CONTINUE

15

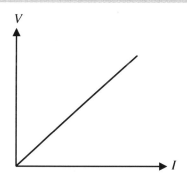

In electricity and magnetism, voltage, V, is the product of current, I and resistance, R. If the graph above represents this relationship, what does the slope of this graph represent?

A) Voltage

B) Current

C) Resistance

D) The product of current and resistance

16

Scientists believe that a certain type of radioactive nuclear waste has its mass reduced by half every 20 years. There are currently 70 kilograms of this type of nuclear waste at a waste management facility. If m represents the mass of nuclear waste in kilograms and t represents the number of years from today, which of the following equations best represents the relationship between m and t?

A) $m = 70(0.5)^{\frac{t}{20}}$

B) $m = 70(0.5)^{20t}$

C) $m = 70 - 70\left(\frac{t}{20}\right)(0.5)$

D) $m = 70 - 20\left(\frac{t}{20}\right)(0.5)$

17

$$-16 < 5 - 3a \le 2$$

If a is an integer, what is the difference between the greatest and least possible value for a?

A) 3

B) 4

C) 5

D) 6

CONTINUE

18

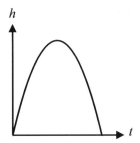

A projectile is launched into the air following the equation of $h(t) = -40t^2 + 200t$, where $h(t)$ is the height of the projectile above the ground in feet, and t is the time, in seconds. How much time elapses, in seconds, from the time the projectile is launched to the time the projectile hits the ground?

A)   1

B)   4

C)   5

D) 16

19

What is the equation of a line that passes through the points $(4, -6)$ and $(-2, 18)$?

A) $y = -\dfrac{1}{4}x + 10$

B) $y = -\dfrac{1}{4}x + 7$

C) $y = -4x + 10$

D) $y = -4x + 7$

20

$$f(x) = x - 3$$
$$5f(x^2) = 2x - 8$$

Two functions of x are shown above. What is the value of x, if x is a non-negative value?

A)   0

B) $\dfrac{5}{7}$

C) $1\dfrac{2}{5}$

D) $2\dfrac{1}{2}$

CONTINUE

21

If y doubles every time x is halved, which of the following graphs could represent the relationship between x and y?

A)

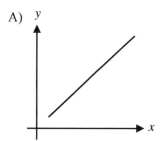

B)

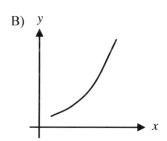

C)

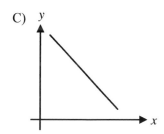

D)

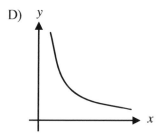

22

A collection of numbers M consists of all positive integers less than 20. If a collection of numbers N is a collection created by randomly choosing five numbers from M, which of the following must be true about N?

    I.   The range must be at least 4.
    II. The median must be at least 3.
    III. The mean can be above 17.

A) I only

B) II only

C) I and II only

D) I and III only

23

An alloy is a mixture of metals. Brass is an alloy made of copper and zinc. A sculptor would like to make a brass sculpture that contains 50% zinc. If copper costs 6 dollars a gram and zinc costs 3 dollars a gram, which equation represents the cost c, in dollars, for the sculptor to make a brass alloy sculpture weighing w grams?

A) $c = w\left(4 + \dfrac{1}{2}\right)$

B) $c = w$

C) $c = 4w$

D) $c = 9w$

CONTINUE

24

$$y - 4 = 4x + 3y = -(9 - x)$$

In the system of linear equations above, what is the value of xy?

A) 0

B) –1

C) –4

D) –6

25

Development of a Bee	
Stage	Duration
Egg	2 days
Larva	1 week
Pupa	5 days
Adult	2 weeks

A honeybee must develop through 4 stages to become a full-grown adult. The length and stages of the bee's development are shown in the table above. In a controlled environment, a queen bee produces new eggs at a constant rate throughout a four-week period. If 200 of these developing bees were randomly selected at the end of this period, how many larvae would we expect to find?

A) 50

B) 75

C) 100

D) 125

26

If the average of c, d, and e is a, then which of the following is the average of b, c, d, and e?

A) $\dfrac{a + b}{3}$

B) $\dfrac{a + b}{4}$

C) $\dfrac{3a + b}{4}$

D) $\dfrac{a + 3b}{3}$

27

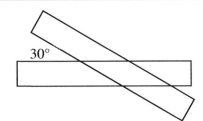

Two pieces of wood overlap at a 30° angle, as shown in the figure above. If the pieces of wood are each 4 cm wide, what is the area of the parallelogram formed by the overlap, in cm²?

A) 8

B) 16

C) 24

D) 32

CONTINUE

DIRECTIONS

Questions **28-31** ask you to solve a problem and enter your answer in the grid provided on your answer sheet. When completing grid-in questions:

1. You are required to bubble in the circles for your answers. It is recommended, but not required, that you also write your answer in the boxes above the columns of circles. Points will be awarded based only on whether the circles are filled in correctly.

2. Fill in only one circle in a column.

3. You can start your answer in any column as long as you can fit in the whole answer.

4. For questions 28-31, no answers will be negative numbers.

5. **Mixed Numbers,** such as $4\frac{2}{5}$, must be gridded as decimals or improper fractions, such as 4.4 or as 22/5. "42/5" will be read as "forty-two over five," not as "four and two-fifths."

6. If your answer is a **decimal** with more digits than will fit on the grid, you may round it or cut it off, but you must fill the entire grid.

7. If there are **multiple correct solutions** to a problem, all of them will be considered correct. Enter only **one** on the grid.

28

If $3^{2x+2} = 27^{x-2}$, what is the value of $x^2 + 1$?

29

Child: **$5**

Adult: **$30**

Senior: **$20**

1 year family membership
(up to 4 family members)
$400

The price of admission to a zoo is presented on the sign above. If the Tremblay family spends $185 on 12 child and adult tickets for one day, how many adults are there in the family?

CONTINUE

Questions 30 and 31 refer to the following information.

Submarines emit a sonar wave, a sound pulse, to detect the presence of obstacles in the water. The speed of a sonar wave is 340 meters per second. The wave travels from the submarine to an object and immediately bounces back. Once it returns, the wave is detected by the submarine. The amount of time from when the wave is emitted to when the wave is detected by the submarine is used to estimate the location of an obstacle.

30

The Seastorm submarine is stationary within the sea. The submarine emits a sonar signal in order to determine how far away it is from a shipwreck. The signal travels to the shipwreck and bounces back to the submarine with no other obstacle in its path. If the signal is detected by the submarine 20 seconds after it is emitted, how far, in kilometers, is the submarine from the shipwreck?

31

The Wayfarer submarine is travelling at a speed of 6 meters per second, and is approaching an island that is 2040 meters away. There is no obstacle between the submarine and the island. If the Wayfarer emits a sonar signal as it approaches the island, how many seconds does it take for the signal to be detected by the submarine? (Round your answer to the nearest tenth of a second.)

STOP

If you complete this section before the end of your allotted time, check your work on this section only. Do NOT use the time to work on another section.

PRACTICE TEST 3

PSAT

Directions

- Work on just one section at a time.
- If you complete a section before the end of your allotted time, use the extra minutes to check your work on that section only. Do NOT use the time to work on another section.

Using Your Test Booklet

- No credit will be given for anything written in the test booklet. You may use the text booklet for scratch paper.
- You are not allowed to continue answering questions in a section after the allotted time has run out. This includes marking answers on your answer sheet that you previously noted in your test booklet.
- You are not allowed to fold pages, take pages out of the test booklet, or take any pages home.

Answering Questions

- Each answer must be marked in the corresponding row on the answer sheet.
- Each bubble must be filled in completely and darkly within the lines.

    Correct ●   Incorrect ⓐ ⊗ ⊘ ⊕ ⊛ Ⓑ ⊜ ⊛

- Be careful to bubble in the correct part of the answer sheet.
- Extra marks on your answer sheet may be marked as incorrect answers and lower your score.
- Make sure you use a No. 2 pencil.

Scoring

- You will receive one point for each correct answer.
- Incorrect answers will NOT result in points deducted. Even if you are unsure about an answer, you should make a guess.

**DO NOT BEGIN THIS TEST
UNTIL YOUR PROCTOR TELLS YOU TO DO SO**

Download printable answer sheets, answer keys, and Excel scoring sheets from:

ivyglobal.com/study

SECTION 4

1 (A) (B) (C) (D)
2 (A) (B) (C) (D)
3 (A) (B) (C) (D)
4 (A) (B) (C) (D)
5 (A) (B) (C) (D)
6 (A) (B) (C) (D)
7 (A) (B) (C) (D)
8 (A) (B) (C) (D)
9 (A) (B) (C) (D)
10 (A) (B) (C) (D)

11 (A) (B) (C) (D)
12 (A) (B) (C) (D)
13 (A) (B) (C) (D)
14 (A) (B) (C) (D)
15 (A) (B) (C) (D)
16 (A) (B) (C) (D)
17 (A) (B) (C) (D)
18 (A) (B) (C) (D)
19 (A) (B) (C) (D)
20 (A) (B) (C) (D)

21 (A) (B) (C) (D)
22 (A) (B) (C) (D)
23 (A) (B) (C) (D)
24 (A) (B) (C) (D)
25 (A) (B) (C) (D)
26 (A) (B) (C) (D)
27 (A) (B) (C) (D)

28

	/	/	
.	.	.	.
	0	0	0
1	1	1	1
2	2	2	2
3	3	3	3
4	4	4	4
5	5	5	5
6	6	6	6
7	7	7	7
8	8	8	8
9	9	9	9

29

	/	/	
.	.	.	.
	0	0	0
1	1	1	1
2	2	2	2
3	3	3	3
4	4	4	4
5	5	5	5
6	6	6	6
7	7	7	7
8	8	8	8
9	9	9	9

30

	/	/	
.	.	.	.
	0	0	0
1	1	1	1
2	2	2	2
3	3	3	3
4	4	4	4
5	5	5	5
6	6	6	6
7	7	7	7
8	8	8	8
9	9	9	9

31

	/	/	
.	.	.	.
	0	0	0
1	1	1	1
2	2	2	2
3	3	3	3
4	4	4	4
5	5	5	5
6	6	6	6
7	7	7	7
8	8	8	8
9	9	9	9

Section 1

Reading Test

60 MINUTES, 47 QUESTIONS

Turn to Section 1 of your answer sheet to answer the questions in this section.

DIRECTIONS

Every passage or paired set of passages is accompanied by a number of questions. Read the passage or paired set of passages, then use what is said or implied in what you read and in any given graphics to choose the best answer to each question.

Questions 1-10 are based on the following passage and supplementary material.

This passage is adapted from Maria Konnikova, "What's Lost as Handwriting Fades." ©2014 by *The New York Times Company*.

Psychologists and neuroscientists say it is too soon to declare handwriting a relic of the past. New evidence suggests that the links between
Line handwriting and broader educational development
5 run deep.

Children not only learn to read more quickly when they first learn to write by hand, but they also remain better able to generate ideas and retain information. In other words, it's not just what we
10 write that matters—but how.

"When we write, a unique neural circuit is automatically activated," said Stanislas Dehaene, a psychologist. "There is a core recognition of the gesture in the written word, a sort of recognition by
15 mental simulation in your brain. It seems that this circuit is contributing in unique ways we didn't realize. Learning is made easier."

A 2012 study lent support to that view. Children who had not yet learned to read and write were
20 presented with a letter or a shape on an index card and asked to reproduce it in one of three ways: trace the image on a page with a dotted outline, draw it on a blank white sheet, or type it on a computer. They

were then placed in a brain scanner and shown the
25 image again.

The researchers found that the initial duplication process mattered. When children had drawn a letter freehand, they exhibited increased activity in areas of the brain that are activated in adults when they
30 read and write. By contrast, children who typed or traced the letter or shape showed no such effect. The activation was significantly weaker.

Dr. James attributes the differences to the messiness inherent in free-form handwriting: not
35 only must we plan and execute the action in a way that is not required when we have a traceable outline, but we are also likely to produce a result that is highly variable. That variability may itself be a learning tool. "When a kid produces a messy letter,"
40 Dr. James said, "that might help him learn it." Our brain must understand that each possible iteration of an "a" is the same, no matter how we see it written. Being able to decipher the messiness of each "a" may be more helpful in establishing that eventual
45 representation than seeing the same result repeatedly.

The effect goes beyond letter recognition. A study that followed children in grades two through five demonstrated that printing, cursive writing, and
50 typing on a keyboard are all associated with separate brain patterns. When the children composed text by hand, they consistently produced more words more

CONTINUE

quickly than they did on a keyboard, and expressed more ideas. And brain imaging
55 suggested that the connection between writing and idea generation went further. When these children were asked to come up with ideas for a composition, the ones with better handwriting exhibited greater neural activation in areas
60 associated with working memory, and increased overall activation in the reading and writing networks.

Two psychologists have reported that in both laboratory settings and classrooms, students learn
65 better when they take notes by hand than when they type on a keyboard. The new research suggests that writing by hand allows the student to process a lecture's contents and reframe it.

Not every expert is persuaded that the long-
70 term benefits of handwriting are all that significant. Still, one such skeptic, psychologist Paul Bloom, says the new research is, at least, thought-provoking. "With handwriting, the very act of putting it down forces you to focus on
75 what's important," he said. He added, after pausing to consider, "Maybe it helps you think better."

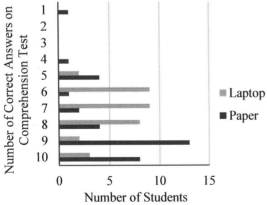

Note-Taking Method and Performance

This data is from a study in which college students took lecture notes either on paper or on a laptop, then took a comprehension test about the content they had just heard.

1

The passage primarily focuses on

A) how the brain develops as children learn to read.

B) the need to limit young adults' use of keyboards.

C) the role that writing by hand plays in learning.

D) the importance of having good handwriting.

2

The passage most strongly suggests that doubts about the findings of the new handwriting research

A) need to be more widely acknowledged by language researchers.

B) are irrelevant and not worth addressing.

C) have not stopped scientists from beginning to take the topic seriously.

D) are widespread among teachers in the United States.

3

Which choice provides the best evidence for the answer to the previous question?

A) Lines 26-27 ("The researchers … mattered")

B) Lines 33-34 ("Dr. James … handwriting")

C) Lines 66-68 ("The new … it")

D) Lines 71-73 ("Still … thought-provoking")

CONTINUE

4

According to the passage, variation in handwritten letters

A) is helpful for ultimately learning to recognize them.

B) is confusing for students learning to read and write.

C) should be eliminated by more handwriting practice in the classroom.

D) leads to increased activation in parts of the brain.

5

Which choice provides the best evidence for the answer to the previous question?

A) Lines 9-10 ("In other … how")

B) Line 18 ("A 2012 … view")

C) Lines 43-46 ("Being able … repeatedly")

D) Lines 47-51 ("A study … patterns")

6

As used in line 8, "generate" most nearly means

A) provoke.

B) produce.

C) promote.

D) precipitate.

7

In lines 11-17, Dr. Dehaene's tone is best described as

A) explanatory.

B) pedantic.

C) demonstrative.

D) zealous.

8

As used in line 18, "lent" most nearly means

A) furnished.

B) loaned.

C) gave.

D) adapted.

9

Which best summarizes lines 47-62?

A) A study suggests that writing by hand and typing are completely unrelated processes.

B) A study suggests that better handwriting is linked to better academic performance.

C) A study suggests that writing by hand enhances mental speed and creativity.

D) A study suggests that children should not type before the fifth grade.

10

It can reasonably be inferred from the passage and the graphic that

A) the way students take notes does not markedly affect how well they retain information.

B) students who write notes by hand do better in school than students who type their notes on laptops.

C) students who take notes by hand demonstrate better understanding than students who type their notes.

D) studies regarding the effects of note-taking method on information retention have been inconclusive.

CONTINUE

Questions 11-20 are based on the following passage and supplementary material.

This passage is adapted from Carl Zimmer, "In a Mother's Milk, Nutrients, and a Message, Too." ©2014 by *The New York Times Company*.

Milk is not just food. Along with nutrients like protein and calcium, milk contains immune factors that protect infants from disease. It hosts microbes,
Line
5 some of which may colonize the guts of babies and help them digest food. Now it turns out milk also contains messages. A new study of monkeys demonstrates that a hormone present in milk, cortisol, can profoundly affect how babies develop. Infant monkeys rely on cortisol to detect the
10 condition of their mothers, the authors suggest, then adjust their growth and even shift their temperaments.

Katie Hinde, a behavioral biologist, and her colleagues studied 108 rhesus macaque mothers
15 nursing infants. The researchers collected samples of milk, measuring how much energy each provided and the cortisol it contained. They also measured how much weight each nursing monkey gained and tracked its behavior.
20 Cortisol is best known as a stress hormone. When cortisol courses through our bodies, it prepares us to handle fearful situations, increasing the brain's consumption of glucose and suppressing the digestive system. The cortisol in a mother's body
25 can also end up in her milk. Babies appear to be sensitive to the hormone as they nurse. Scientists found that drinking milk causes infants to build receptors in their intestines for detecting cortisol. The same shift doesn't happen when babies drink
30 formula.

Among the macaques, some mothers delivered a lot of cortisol to their babies, while others delivered a little. High-cortisol milk made babies put on weight faster, and they were more nervous and less
35 confident. To make sense of these results, the scientists looked for factors that might determine how much cortisol a mother produced in her milk.

One stood out: how many other offspring she had. New mothers had high cortisol levels in their milk.
40 Hormone levels were much lower in mothers who had had about 10 babies.

When female monkeys start having babies, they can't store as much energy in their milk. New mothers are still small, so their bodies can't provide
45 many of the raw ingredients for milk. Their mammary glands are also underdeveloped, so they can't convert those ingredients efficiently into milk. Monkey mothers who have had more babies are able to supply new infants with more energy. Dr. Hinde
50 suspects that the cortisol that newer mothers give their babies serves as a warning that they shouldn't expect a lot of milk, or energy. She sums up the message: "Prioritize growth, kiddo. You can't really afford to be exploratory and playful. Once you spend
55 a calorie on that, it's a calorie you can't use to grow." The babies fed high-cortisol milk develop a nervous temperament, focusing their limited energy on putting on weight. They grow faster, despite getting less energy from their inexperienced
60 mothers.

Cortisol in breast milk may influence human infants as well. But Melissa Thompson, an anthropologist, cautioned that the differences between monkeys and humans make comparisons
65 difficult. Infant monkeys, for example, cling to their mothers and nurse whenever they want. Human mothers balance breast-feeding with many other tasks. "We should expect the relationship between maternal stress, breast milk and infant temperament
70 in humans to be relatively complex," said Dr. Thompson.

CONTINUE

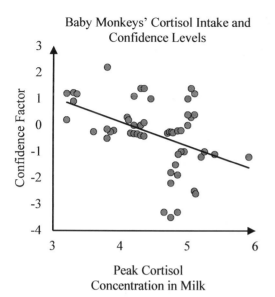

Baby Monkeys' Cortisol Intake and
Confidence Levels

Peak Cortisol
Concentration in Milk

11

The passage primarily focuses on which of the
following aspects of mothers' milk?

A) The nutrients it provides to babies

B) The hormonal signals it facilitates between
mothers and babies

C) The myriad ways it benefits the digestive
systems of babies

D) The effects it has on mothers' moods and
stress levels

12

The passage serves primarily to

A) present and interpret the findings of a new
study.

B) relay a perspective on a hotly-debated
controversy.

C) announce and celebrate the achievement of a
research scientist and her team.

D) further a debate by adding evidence from a
new study to the discussion.

13

The passage most strongly suggests that

A) human breast milk is complex and not
completely understood.

B) infant formula needs to be improved.

C) mothers should try to decrease their stress and
cortisol levels.

D) research findings about monkeys are irrelevant
to humans.

14

Which choice provides the best evidence for the
answer to the previous question?

A) Lines 26-28 ("Scientists found … cortisol")

B) Lines 35-37 ("To make … milk")

C) Lines 48-49 ("Monkey mothers … energy")

D) Lines 68-71 ("We should … Thompson")

15

As used in line 3, "hosts" most nearly means

A) welcomes.

B) contains.

C) moderates.

D) receives.

16

As used in line 21, "courses" most nearly means

A) tracks.

B) pours.

C) flows.

D) rolls.

CONTINUE

17

According to the passage, what is the relationship between cortisol and the health of baby monkeys?

A) The faster baby monkeys grow, the more cortisol they will receive from their mothers.

B) The less cortisol baby monkeys receive from their mothers, the more likely they are to be even-tempered.

C) The more cortisol baby monkeys receive from their mothers, the weaker their immune systems will be.

D) The less cortisol baby monkeys receive, the greater their physical strength will be.

18

Which choice provides the best evidence for the answer to the previous question?

A) Lines 33-35 ("High-cortisol … confident")

B) Line 39 ("New mothers … milk")

C) Lines 49-52 ("Dr. Hinde suspects … energy")

D) Lines 61-62 ("Cortisol in … well")

19

Dr. Thompson would probably agree that the research on baby monkeys

A) suggests important ideas about human development.

B) should be taken into account by companies that make baby formulas.

C) is interesting but not necessarily directly relevant to human babies.

D) was not conducted very well and should be ignored.

20

According to the passage and the graphic

A) baby monkeys who consumed milk with less cortisol became less confident over time.

B) baby monkeys who consumed milk with higher cortisol levels generally exhibited more confident behavior than baby monkeys who consumed milk with lower cortisol levels.

C) baby monkeys who consumed milk with lower cortisol levels generally exhibited more confident behavior than baby monkeys who consumed milk with higher cortisol levels.

D) the cortisol concentration in mother monkeys' milk decreased over time.

CONTINUE

Questions 21-29 are based on the following passage.

This passage is adapted from a speech given in 1920 by lawyer and activist Crystal Eastman after the ratification of the 19th Amendment, which gave women the right to vote.

In fighting for the right to vote most women have tried to be either non-committal or thoroughly respectable on every other subject. Now they can say what they are really after; and what they are after, in common with all the rest of the struggling world, is freedom.

What is the problem of women's freedom? It seems to me to be this: how to arrange the world so that women can be human beings, with a chance to exercise their infinitely varied gifts in infinitely varied ways, instead of being destined by the accident of their sex to one field of activity—housework and child-raising. Second, if and when they choose housework and child-raising, to have that occupation recognized by the world as work, requiring a definite economic reward and not merely entitling the performer to be dependent on some man.

This is not the whole of feminism, of course, but it is enough to begin with. "Oh, don't begin with economics," my friends protest. "Woman does not live by bread alone. What she needs first of all is a free soul." I can agree that women will never be great until they achieve a certain emotional freedom, a strong healthy egotism, and some un-personal sources of joy—that in this inner sense we cannot make woman free by changing her economic status. What we can do is to create conditions of outward freedom in which a free woman's soul can be born and grow. It is these outward conditions with which an organized feminist movement must concern itself.

Freedom of choice in occupation and individual economic independence for women: how shall we approach this next feminist objective? First, by breaking down all remaining barriers, actual as well as legal, which make it difficult for women to enter or succeed in the various professions, to go into and get on in business, to learn trades and practice them, to join trades unions. Chief among these remaining barriers is inequality in pay.

Second, we must institute a revolution in the early training and education of both boys and girls. It must be womanly as well as manly to earn your own living, to stand on your own feet. And it must be manly as well as womanly to know how to cook and sew and clean and take care of yourself in the ordinary exigencies of life. I need not add that the second part of this revolution will be more passionately resisted than the first.

As far as we can see ahead people will always want homes, and a happy home cannot be had without a certain amount of rather monotonous work and responsibility. How can we change the nature of man so that he will honorably share that work and responsibility and thus make the homemaking enterprise a song instead of a burden? Fundamentally it is a problem of early training—we must bring up feminist sons.

But is there any way of ensuring a woman's economic independence while child-raising is her chosen occupation? It seems that the only way we can keep mothers free, at least in a capitalist society, is by the establishment of a principle that the occupation of raising children is peculiarly and directly a service to society, and that the mother upon whom the necessity and privilege of performing this service naturally falls is entitled to an adequate economic reward from the government. It is idle to talk of real economic independence for women unless this principle is accepted. But with a generous endowment of motherhood provided by legislation, with the feminist ideal of education accepted in home and school, and with all special barriers removed in every field of human activity, there is no reason why woman should not become almost a human thing.

CONTINUE

21

The author of this passage primarily aims to

A) celebrate progress towards gender equality.

B) outline further goals that must be achieved for gender equality.

C) berate those who stifle the progress of gender equality.

D) call those who ignore the need for gender equality to act.

22

Which of the following situations is most analogous to the historical moment presented in the passage?

A) A band of adventurers already far from home have the endurance to travel an even greater distance.

B) An underdog politician surprises critics by having the foresight to prepare well for the future.

C) A group of workers wins the right to unionize, enabling them to begin further negotiations.

D) A battered troop of soldiers is unprepared for an enemy ambush.

23

Which choice provides the best evidence for the answer to the previous question?

A) Lines 3-6 ("Now they … freedom")

B) Lines 22-23 ("What she … soul")

C) Lines 34-37 ("First by … professions")

D) Lines 59-61 ("But is … occupation")

24

As used in line 15, "recognized" most nearly means

A) remembered.

B) placed.

C) realized.

D) acknowledged.

25

The author most strongly suggests that

A) women are predisposed to certain careers more than others.

B) women should not be content taking care of children at home.

C) women are capable of pursuing diverse occupations.

D) men are less naturally suited to take care of children than women.

26

Which choice provides the best evidence for the answer to the previous question?

A) Lines 1-3 ("In fighting … subject")

B) Lines 7-11 ("It seems … ways")

C) Lines 28-30 ("What we … grow")

D) Lines 44-47 ("And it … life")

CONTINUE

27

In lines 35-36, what is the most likely reason Eastman makes the distinction, "actual as well as legal?"

A) To demonstrate how the legal system affects women on a daily basis

B) To list the specific types of discouragement women face when trying to gain success in the workplace

C) To indicate that there are factors that inhibit women's success in the workplace other than laws

D) To imply that having children makes it difficult to gain traction in a career

28

In the context of the passage, the author's use of the word "song" (line 56) is primarily meant to

A) propose that singing songs while performing daily chores will make the activity more appealing.

B) suggest that equitable homemaking could be as light and harmonious as a song.

C) compare homemaking to a performance which requires training and rehearsal.

D) ask a rhetorical question which illustrates the magnitude of the challenges ahead.

29

The author's attitude in lines 75-76 is best described as

A) righteous.

B) sardonic.

C) delighted.

D) skeptical.

CONTINUE

Questions 30-38 are based on the following passages.

Passage 1 is adapted from Gina Solomon, "Agent Orange in Your Backyard: The Harmful Pesticide 2,4-D." ©2012 by *The Atlantic Monthly Group*. Passage 2 is adapted from Andrew Pollack, "Paper Tying Rat Cancer to Herbicide is Retracted." ©2013 by *The New York Times Company*.

Passage 1

This weekend, I walked the aisles of a home supply store. On the shelves were an array of weed killers and "weed and feed" products marketed to
Line　keep your lawn looking great. I was hunting for a
5　pesticide known as 2,4-D.

I found it—in several different products. 2,4-D was invented in the chemical boom during World War II, making it one of the oldest pesticides that's still legally on the market today. It was one of the
10　two active ingredients in Agent Orange, the notorious Vietnam War defoliant. Despite decades of studies showing links to lymphoma in humans and dogs, this chemical thrives as one of the top three pesticides sold in the United States today.
15　Newer science shows that it's not just a cancer problem; this pesticide interferes with several essential hormones, thereby increasing the risks of birth defects and neurologic damage in children. Studies in wheat-growing areas where 2,4-D is
20　heavily used have shown increased rates of certain birth defects.

Many people don't realize that many weed and feed products contain a toxic pesticide. People also don't realize that after they apply the product to their
25　lawn, the chemical residues are tracked indoors on shoes or pet paws, and contaminate the carpets. Because 2,4-D is broken down by direct sunlight, once the residues get into the house the pesticide lingers for months or even years. Kids who play on
30　the floor are at particular risk, since they accidentally ingest the chemical when they put their hands in their mouths.

2,4-D is used on athletic fields, golf courses, landscaping, timber land, and crops. The airborne
35　chemical can even travel significant distances,

damaging plants downwind, and contaminating homes. The Natural Resources Defense Council petitioned the Environmental Protection Agency to cancel registrations for 2,4-D. The EPA still hasn't
40　responded, so the NRDC filed a lawsuit against the agency for its delay on this important issue.

Passage 2

A food safety journal has retracted a paper that seemed to show that genetically modified corn and the herbicide Roundup can cause cancer and
45　premature death in rats. The editor of the journal said in a letter to the paper's author that the study's results, while not incorrect, were "inconclusive, and therefore do not reach the threshold of publication."

The paper has been cited by opponents of biotech
50　foods and proponents of labeling such foods. But it has been criticized as flawed, sensationalistic and possibly even fraudulent by many scientists, some allied with the biotechnology industry. The main author of the study, Gilles-Eric Séralini, had done
55　other studies challenging the safety of genetically engineered foods, some of which had also been questioned.

In his letter to Dr. Séralini, the editor of the journal, A. Wallace Hayes, said that "unequivocally"
60　he had found "no evidence of fraud or intentional misrepresentation of the data." However, he said there was "legitimate cause for concern" that the number of rats in the study was too small and that the strain of rat used was prone to cancer. That made
65　it difficult to rule out that the results were not explained by "normal variability," he said.

The study followed 200 rats for two years. The rats that ate either the corn or the Roundup tended to have more tumors and die earlier than the 20 rats in
70　the control group, which were fed nonengineered corn and plain water.

Dr. Séralini and other scientists defended the paper in letters to the journal. They said the same strain of rats was used in a 90-day feeding study that
75　led to European approval of the corn. They also said that even though the rats had a high natural rate of

CONTINUE

cancer, what mattered was the difference in tumor incidence between the rats fed the corn or herbicide and the controls.

30

The author of Passage 1 would most likely agree that

A) the need to protect people from the harmful effects of 2,4-D has not yet been adequately addressed.

B) the benefits of using 2,4-D outweigh the drawbacks of doing so.

C) 2,4-D should only be used in some parts of the country.

D) there should be a complete ban on the manufacture of all chemical pesticides.

31

Which choice provides the best evidence for the answer to the previous question?

A) Lines 2-4 ("On the … great")

B) Line 6 ("I found … products")

C) Lines 29-32 ("Kids who … mouths")

D) Lines 39-41 ("The EPA … issue")

32

As used in line 29, "lingers" most nearly means

A) dawdles.

B) remains.

C) dwells.

D) protracts.

33

Which of the following best describes the structure of Passage 2?

A) A description of a scientific study and the results of the study

B) A presentation of a decision with an explanation of why the decision was made

C) An informative essay with hypotheses about future events

D) A dialog expressing multiple conflicting points of view

34

As used in line 65, "rule out" is closest in meaning to

A) exclude the possibility.

B) include the possibility.

C) ignore the possibility.

D) ascertain the possibility.

35

Based on the information in Passage 2, which of the following changes to the design of the study would best address the concerns expressed by A. Wallace Hayes?

A) Instituting careful oversight to eliminate any possibility that Dr. Séralini's team might falsify or misinterpret data

B) Using a larger population of rats to help rule out natural variability as the source of the findings

C) More carefully calculating the difference in tumor incidence to control for the rats' high natural rates of cancer

D) Removing any rats that develop tumors naturally from the experiment

CONTINUE

36

Which choice provides the best evidence for the answer to the previous question?

A) Lines 58-61 ("In his … data")

B) Lines 61-64 ("However, he … cancer")

C) Lines 67 ("The study … years")

D) Lines 73-75 ("They said … corn")

37

What is the relationship between Passages 1 and 2?

A) Passage 1 makes claims about an herbicide and Passage 2 negates those claims.

B) Passage 1 reports the dangers of an herbicide and Passage 2 reports doubt regarding a study about another herbicide.

C) Passage 1 addresses the concerns about herbicides presented in Passage 2.

D) Passage 1 discusses the drawbacks of an herbicide and Passage 2 discusses the drawbacks of an alternative herbicide.

38

Passage 1 and Passage 2 both discuss

A) the possible health dangers of herbicides.

B) individuals affected by herbicides.

C) action being taken to counteract the effects of herbicides.

D) scientists who study the effects of herbicides.

CONTINUE

Questions 39-47 are based on the following passage.

This passage is adapted from Robert Louis Stevenson, "The Adventure of the Hansom Cabs," originally published in 1878. Brackenbury is a lieutenant who has recently returned to London.

The night was already advanced when a plump of cold rain fell suddenly out of the darkness. Brackenbury caught sight of a hansom cabman making him a sign that he was disengaged. The circumstance fell in so happily to the occasion that he at once raised his cane in answer, and had soon ensconced himself in the London gondola.

"Where to, sir?" asked the driver.

"Where you please," said Brackenbury.

And immediately, at a pace of surprising swiftness, the hansom drove off through the rain into a maze of villas. There was so little to distinguish the deserted lamp-lit streets through which the flying hansom took its way that Brackenbury soon lost all idea of direction.

He would have been tempted to believe that the cabman was amusing himself by driving him round and round about a small quarter, but there was something business-like in the speed which convinced him of the contrary. The man had an object in view—he was hastening towards a definite end; and Brackenbury was at once astonished at the fellow's skill in picking a way through such a labyrinth, and a little concerned to imagine the occasion of his hurry. Did the driver belong to some treacherous association? And was he himself being whirled to a murderous death?

The thought had scarcely presented itself, when the cab swung sharply round a corner and pulled up before the garden gate of a villa. The house was brilliantly lighted up. Another hansom had just driven away, and Brackenbury could see a gentleman being admitted at the front door and received by several servants. He was surprised that the cabman should have stopped so immediately in front of a house where a reception was being held;

he did not doubt it was the result of accident, and sat placidly where he was, until he heard the trap thrown open over his head.

"Here we are, sir," said the driver.

"Here!" repeated Brackenbury. "Where?"

"You told me to take you where I pleased, sir," returned the man with a chuckle, "and here we are."

It struck Brackenbury that the voice was smooth and courteous for a man in so inferior a position; he remembered the speed at which he had been driven; and now it occurred to him that the hansom was more luxuriously appointed than the common run of public conveyances.

"I must ask you to explain," said he. "Do you mean to turn me out into the rain? My good man, I suspect the choice is mine."

"The choice is certainly yours," replied the driver; "but when I tell you all, I believe I know how a gentleman of your figure will decide. There is a gentlemen's party in this house. I do not know whether the master be a stranger to London and without acquaintances of his own; or whether he is a man of odd notions. But certainly I was hired to kidnap single gentlemen in evening dress. You have simply to go in and say that Mr. Morris invited you."

"Are you Mr. Morris?" inquired the Lieutenant.

"Oh, no," replied the cabman. "Mr. Morris is the person of the house."

"It is not a common way of collecting guests," said Brackenbury: "but an eccentric man might very well indulge the whim without any intention to offend. Suppose that I refuse Mr. Morris's invitation," he went on, "what then?"

"My orders are to drive you back where I took you from," replied the man, "and set out to look for others. Those who have no fancy for such an adventure, Mr. Morris said, were not the guests for him."

These words decided the Lieutenant on the spot.

"After all," he reflected, as he descended from the hansom, "I have not had long to wait for my adventure."

CONTINUE

39

The passage primarily focuses on

A) Brackenbury's evolving nature.

B) the unusual events of an evening.

C) Brackenbury's personal history.

D) the curious life of the cabman.

40

Over the course of the passage, the main focus of the narrative shifts from a

A) character's fear of the unknown to a character's new excitement about taking risks.

B) description of a lonely character to a depiction of a joyful community.

C) character's aimlessness to a character's bold decision.

D) meditation on the need for stimulation to an ode to security.

41

Brackenbury decided to get into the cab because he

A) wanted to ride around the countryside.

B) wanted to get out of the rain.

C) had been expecting just such an adventure.

D) needed to get to a party.

42

Which choice provides the best evidence for the answer to the previous question?

A) Lines 3-4 ("Brackenbury caught … disengaged")

B) Lines 4-7 ("The circumstance … gondola")

C) Lines 10-12 ("And immediately … villas")

D) Lines 28-30 ("The thought … villa")

43

Which of the following choices best describes the interactions between Brackenbury and the cabman?

A) Cold, due to irreconcilable differences

B) Cordial, despite a peculiar situation

C) Adversarial, in light of a conflict of interests

D) Intimate, as a result of a shared experience

44

The rhetorical effect of the word "flying" in line 13 is to

A) indicate that the wheels of the cab occasionally lifted off the pavement.

B) suggest that Brackenbury is comparing the cab to an airplane.

C) describe the cab as traveling very quickly.

D) demonstrate Brackenbury's fear to the reader.

CONTINUE

45

As used in line 75, "decided" most nearly means

A) chose.

B) convinced.

C) answered.

D) adjudicated.

46

The passage most strongly suggests that Brackenbury will

A) attend the party.

B) search for adventure elsewhere.

C) seek revenge against the cab driver.

D) return to downtown London.

47

Which choice provides the best evidence for the answer to the previous question?

A) Lines 68-69 ("Suppose that … then")

B) Lines 70-72 ("My orders … others")

C) Lines 72-74 ("Those who … him")

D) Lines 76-78 ("After all … adventure")

STOP

If you complete this section before the end of your allotted time, check your work on this section only. Do NOT use the time to work on another section.

Section 2

Writing and Language Test

35 MINUTES, 44 QUESTIONS

Turn to Section 2 of your answer sheet to answer the questions in this section.

DIRECTIONS

Every passage comes with a set of questions. Some questions will ask you to consider how the writer might revise the passage to improve the expression of ideas. Other questions will ask you to consider correcting potential errors in sentence structure, usage, or punctuation. There may be one or more graphics that you will need to consult as you revise and edit the passage.

Some questions will refer to a portion of the passage that has been underlined. Other questions will refer to a particular spot in a passage or ask that you consider the passage in full.

After you read the passage, select the answers to questions that most effectively improve the passage's writing quality or that adjust the passage to follow the conventions of standard written English. Many questions give you the option to select "NO CHANGE." Select that option in cases where you think the relevant part of the passage should remain as it currently is.

Questions 1-11 are based on the following passage.

The Search for Other Worlds

One of the most exciting frontiers in astronomy is the study of planets outside our solar system. Though these *exoplanets* orbit distant stars that humans may never **1** visit. They are of great interest to any scientists and members of the general public who want to know if other worlds may harbor life. Despite the scientific value in finding and studying exoplanets, few governments provide enough funding for this type of astronomical research. More attention should be paid to this important line of scientific inquiry.

1

A) NO CHANGE
B) visit: they
C) visit. However, they
D) visit, they

CONTINUE

2 [1] Because they are usually too distant and dim to be spotted and photographed directly, exoplanets must often be detected by indirect techniques. [2] However, both of these techniques rely on high-quality observations of stars. [3] One such technique is the *transit method*, which finds planets by spotting the changes in brightness they cause when they pass in front of the stars they orbit. [4] Another is the *radial velocity method*, which notes small movements of stars caused by the gravity of an orbiting planet. [5] When scientists applied these methods to observations from Earth-bound telescopes, which are limited by interference from the atmosphere, they **3** find only "hot Jupiters." [6] These enormous planets have orbits much smaller **4** than Earth, and are unlikely to be hospitable to life. **5**

2

Which choice most effectively expresses the main topic of this paragraph?

A) Many exoplanets have unusual characteristics that make them very unlike Earth.

B) Scientists use a variety of methods to find exoplanets.

C) Only a few astronomers have the expertise needed to identify exoplanets.

D) Other astronomical objects can often be confused with exoplanets.

3

A) NO CHANGE

B) are finding

C) would find

D) found

4

A) NO CHANGE

B) than Earth's

C) than Earth is

D) than the Earth

5

To make this paragraph most logical, sentence 2 should be placed

A) where it is now.

B) after sentence 3.

C) after sentence 4.

D) after sentence 6.

CONTINUE

In the hopes of finding more Earth-like exoplanets, the National Aeronautics and Space Administration (NASA) launched an orbital telescope called Kepler **6** that was launched in order to make better observations of stars in our galaxy. This mission was extraordinarily successful; Kepler enabled hundreds of exoplanets to be detected by the transit method in 2014. Based on **7** it's findings, scientists estimated that as many as 40 billion potentially habitable Earth-sized planets could exist in our galaxy.

However, the Kepler mission has been consistently **8** ravaged by problems due to NASA's limited funding. The project was delayed several times before the telescope's **9** launch, as a result of funding cuts. In addition, mechanical failures have damaged Kepler in orbit, crippling its ability to rotate and endangering its mission to collect data.

6

A) NO CHANGE
B) that was launched for
C) to make
D) make

7

A) NO CHANGE
B) its
C) their
D) they're

8

A) NO CHANGE
B) defiled
C) plagued
D) disfigured

9

A) NO CHANGE
B) launch: as a
C) launch; as a
D) launch as a

CONTINUE

This is hardly surprising given the budget cuts NASA has suffered. **10** In the past, when the US government made space exploration a higher priority, NASA used its ample funding to produce valuable new technologies and important scientific findings. Moreover, NASA's highly visible accomplishments, including landing astronauts on the moon in 1969, inspired a generation of **11** scientists so more support for NASA in its mission to find exoplanets would deliver untold benefits to science and to the American people.

10

The writer wants to include a sentence that provides evidence that NASA's budget problems are a result of changing government priorities. Which choice would best accomplish this goal?

A) NASA's budget as a percentage of the United States federal budget has decreased eightfold since the 1960s.

B) Like any government agency, sometimes NASA has to balance its objectives against its available budget.

C) NASA needed $17 million to be able to really explore the existence of exoplanets.

D) The U.S. federal government needs to provide NASA with enough money to launch successful missions.

11

A) NO CHANGE

B) scientists. So more

C) scientists, so more

D) scientists. More

CONTINUE

Questions 12-22 are based on the following passage.

Haruki Murakami and the Literature of Japan

Haruki Murakami is one of Japan's best-known authors. In a career spanning almost 40 years, he has produced an enormous body of work including [12] <u>novels, and short stories, and nonfiction</u>. Many of his works have been translated into languages other than Japanese and are popular internationally.

Murakami began writing at the age of 29. Though he had never before been [13] <u>aspired</u> to write, he was suddenly struck with the idea that he could and should write a novel. His first few novels, published in the early 1980s, were moderately successful, but Murakami did not become widely known until several years later, with the release of *Norwegian Wood* in 1987. This novel explored the lives and relationships of a group of Japanese college students. It was immensely popular with young readers both in Japan and abroad and is considered Murakami's breakout work.

12

A) NO CHANGE

B) novels and short stories, and nonfiction

C) novels, and short stories, nonfiction

D) novels, short stories, and nonfiction

13

A) NO CHANGE

B) inspired

C) conspired

D) transpired

CONTINUE

[1] Murakami's more recent works **14** are viewed as really good by readers and critics due to their unique style and subject matter. [2] For instance, his novel *Kafka on the Shore* features an elderly man who can talk to cats and a teenage runaway who stumbles into the afterlife while still alive. [3] Many of his novels and stories feature characters who are outsiders in Japanese society, lacking steady jobs or strong social ties. [4] For example, the protagonists of his novel *After Dark* are Mari, a loner and student, and Takahashi, a slacker and jazz musician. **15** [5] Such characters allow Murakami to criticize conformist aspects of Japanese culture and **16** he also explores themes of isolation and alienation. [6] Murakami is also well known for his use of magical realism, a literary style that blends fantastical and surreal elements with the everyday. [7] These stylistic flourishes give his work a distinctive flavor. **17**

14

A) are liked a lot by

B) have earned praise from

C) get a lot of love from

D) are super popular with

15

The author is considering adding a sentence that emphasizes Murakami's use of outsiders as characters. Which choice would best accomplish this goal?

A) Several of the other characters in *After Dark*, such as the night hotel owner Kaoru, are also on the margins of Japanese society.

B) However, the main character of his novel *Sputnik Sweetheart* holds a respectable job.

C) Murakami drew on his experience as the former owner of a jazz club to write about Takahashi's love of jazz.

D) Similarly, an increasing number of Japanese youth find themselves without secure jobs.

16

A) NO CHANGE

B) also exploring

C) explore

D) exploration of

17

To make this paragraph most logical, sentence 2 should be placed

A) where it is now.

B) after sentence 3.

C) before sentence 5.

D) before sentence 7.

CONTINUE →

18 Some of his fellow Japanese authors criticize the strong influence of Western culture on his work. For instance, his work contains numerous references to Western jazz and classical **19** <u>music. He also pays little attention</u> to classical Japanese culture.

18

Which choice most effectively conveys the main topic of this paragraph?

A) Murakami's writing draws from an eclectic set of influences and sources.

B) Additional criticisms of Murakami's novels focus on cultural issues.

C) However, Murakami's writing has attracted criticism as well.

D) Japanese history and current events have informed much of Murakami's work.

19

Which choice most effectively contrasts the emphasis given to Western and Japanese culture in Murakami's work?

A) NO CHANGE

B) music, although he pays a little attention

C) music, with little attention paid

D) music. However, he also alludes

CONTINUE

Murakami's novels and nonfiction have also, at times, addressed controversial topics. His novel *The Wind-up Bird Chronicle*, for example, discusses war crimes committed by Japan during [20] World War II; considered a delicate subject by many. His nonfiction work *Underground,* which contains interviews with people affected by a domestic terrorist attack on a Tokyo subway in 1995, was also somewhat contentious. Some thought this book was harshly [21] critical to Japan's culture and media. [22] In light of such criticisms, Murakami remains highly popular in Japan and to this day enjoys an enormous readership and international acclaim.

20

A) NO CHANGE

B) World War II, considered

C) World War II: considered

D) World War II considered

21

A) NO CHANGE

B) critical in

C) critical at

D) critical of

22

A) NO CHANGE

B) In spite of

C) Irrespective of

D) In addition to

CONTINUE

Questions 23-33 are based on the following passage.

Ignaz Semmelweis, Pioneer of Modern Medicine

The development of modern medicine was a long and slow process. Doctors and other caregivers accumulated knowledge by fits and starts, and in many cases, important breakthroughs **23** took a pretty long time to get noticed. No story demonstrates this better than that of Ignaz Semmelweis, a Hungarian doctor whose contributions to our modern understanding of disease **24** are known to far too few people today.

After completing his medical studies at the University of Vienna in 1844, Semmelweis went to work in the Vienna General Hospital. There, he was a specialist in *obstetrics*, focusing on caring for pregnant women and delivering **25** their child. At that time, childbirth was more dangerous for mothers than it is today; some women died from infections that doctors did not know how to treat.

23
A) NO CHANGE
B) took absolutely forever to be noticed
C) went unnoticed for many years
D) languished in utter obscurity

24
A) NO CHANGE
B) being
C) was
D) is

25
A) NO CHANGE
B) the child
C) their children
D) the children

CONTINUE

Semmelweis noticed that new mothers were much more likely to die of infection after giving birth in the hospital's First Clinic than in the Second Clinic. Applying scientific reasoning, he collected data on the two clinics and set about trying to determine the reason for the **26** divergence. He realized that the First Clinic employed medical students, who performed autopsies, while the Second Clinic employed midwives, who **27** did not perform any autopsies. Concluding that the medical students were infecting new mothers with "cadaverous particles," **28** the medical students were ordered by Semmelweis to wash their hands before delivering infants. As a result, the First Clinic's mortality rate dropped dramatically.

26

A) NO CHANGE
B) bifurcation
C) difference
D) departure

27

A) NO CHANGE
B) did not perform autopsies
C) did not perform any
D) did not

28

A) NO CHANGE
B) Semmelweis ordered the medical students to wash their hands
C) hand washing was ordered for the medical students by Semmelweis
D) the medical students washed their hands, by order of Semmelweis,

CONTINUE

29 [1] The prevailing belief among medical professionals was that diseases were caused by exposure to "bad air" and imbalances in levels of certain bodily fluids. [2] Doctors at that time were totally unaware of the role that bacteria and viruses play in transmitting disease. [3] The medical community thus **30** deluded Semmelweis's ideas about "cadaverous particles" as unscientific. [4] Semmelweis expressed more and more outrage as other doctors ignored his results, and was eventually accused of having gone insane. [5] Some doctors also felt insulted by his suggestion that they might have been "unclean" in some way. [6] He died in 1865 shortly after being committed to an asylum. **31**

29

Which choice most effectively establishes the main topic of this paragraph?

A) Soon, the First Clinic was just as safe as the Second Clinic for new mothers.

B) Semmelweis wondered what the nature of these so-called "cadaverous particles" might be.

C) The practice of hand washing took a long time to catch on at other hospitals.

D) Unfortunately, the wider community of doctors and scientists refused to accept Semmelweis's findings.

30

A) NO CHANGE

B) diluted

C) denuded

D) derided

31

To make the order of this paragraph most logical, sentence 5 should be placed

A) where it is now.

B) after sentence 1.

C) before sentence 3.

D) after sentence 6.

CONTINUE

Of course, we know today that Semmelweis's method for preventing infection was effective and vitally important. Later scientists built on Semmelweis's understanding to help reduce mortality from infections. Sadly, these later scientists and their discoveries have overshadowed Semmelweis's name and accomplishments. For example, **32** Louis <u>Pasteur helped</u> discover the role of bacteria and viruses in disease. **33** Semmelweis's discoveries about basic sanitation prefigure such contributions, and he deserves to be remembered alongside other pioneers of modern medicine as a savior of millions of lives.

32

A) NO CHANGE

B) Pasteur who helped

C) Pasteur: who helped

D) Pasteur helping

33

The writer wants to include a second example that supports the claim that Semmelweis's method was overshadowed by discoveries by other researchers. Which choice most effectively accomplishes this goal?

A) Pasteur also invented the process of "pasteurization," a technique still used today to keep food and beverages from spoiling.

B) Joseph Lister developed antiseptic techniques to clean surgical instruments, making surgery safer for patients.

C) Unfortunately, mortality rates from post-childbirth infections are still relatively high in much of the developing world.

D) That is why, nowadays, hand sanitizer is commercially available and can be found almost anywhere in the United States.

CONTINUE

Questions 34-44 are based on the following passage.

Directing: Where Performance and Visual Arts Meet

Directors play a crucial role in the fields of theater and film. These professionals work to develop a creative vision for a movie or stage production and turn that vision into reality. Though this is a difficult and complex task, directors enjoy both the reward of seeing their ideas realized and the acclaim that successful productions earn.

What skills do directors need to succeed in **34** their work. First, **35** one needs to be able to read and interpret fiction. Their first task is always to analyze the script of a film or play and determine how best to bring it to life. In order to do this, directors must be skilled in understanding the intentions of authors and recognizing the **36** refinements in their writing.

In addition, directors must **37** really have it together. They usually coordinate the many different aspects of a production. In theater, this may include overseeing set design, orchestral performance, and arrangements for lighting and sound. In film, directors must also consider how best to shoot their films, edit them into their final forms, and score them with music.

34

A) NO CHANGE
B) their work!
C) their work…
D) their work?

35

A) NO CHANGE
B) he or she needs
C) you need
D) they need

36

A) NO CHANGE
B) suggestions
C) nuances
D) shadows

37

A) NO CHANGE
B) be really on top of everything
C) be highly organized
D) really have everything organized

CONTINUE

Finally, directors need to be good at communicating and working with **38** other's. They work with large crews that are responsible for the technical aspects of a production, and must be able to give these crews clear and effective instructions. Directors must also instruct actors in order to **39** be ensured that they give the best performances possible. **40** Furthermore, directors are sometimes required to be the public face of a production, especially in theater and "art house" film. As a result, their ability to communicate with the press about their work is very important. **41** Often, directors will hire other professionals to choose actors who seem like they would be suited for the part.

38

A) NO CHANGE
B) others'
C) others
D) others's

39

A) NO CHANGE
B) ensure
C) be sure
D) be certain to

40

A) NO CHANGE
B) Even so,
C) Without a doubt,
D) Despite this,

41

The writer is considering deleting the underlined sentence to improve the focus of the passage. Should the underlined sentence be kept or deleted?

A) Kept, because it supports the claim that directors must handle communications with many different people in many different roles.

B) Kept, because it helps establish the claim that directing requires organization, attention to detail, and flexibility.

C) Deleted, because it distracts from the paragraph's central claim that directors should have strong communication skills.

D) Deleted, because the sentence does not specify what sort of professionals directors may hire to assist in the casting process.

CONTINUE

There is no formal educational requirement to begin working as a director, but the field is very competitive. Aspiring directors may benefit from undergraduate and graduate degrees in film, drama, or related fields. While pursuing degrees, it's a good idea to seek out additional opportunities to build practical skills and **42** making connections in the field. Many directors work on small shows or films independently before beginning their degree program, or in addition to their coursework. **43**

Aspiring directors should be passionate about the work of directing itself. The career is challenging, and the field is highly competitive. For those who love the **44** work, while directing can be a fulfilling career: creative, engaging, and rewarding.

42

A) NO CHANGE

B) made

C) will make

D) make

43

The writer is considering inserting a sentence to support the claim that working on productions independently of degree programs can be beneficial for directors' careers. Which choice would best accomplish that goal?

A) The requirements of stage and film projects are very different, even on small-scale productions.

B) Small-scale, low-cost projects can be a fulfilling experience for artists and audiences alike.

C) Building a portfolio of projects and a network of colleagues early on can help directors to secure further work in their field.

D) Working as assistant directors on larger projects can also be an excellent opportunity for aspiring directors to learn the craft of directing.

44

A) NO CHANGE

B) work, though, directing

C) work, and directing

D) work, but directing

STOP

If you complete this section before the end of your allotted time, check your work on this section only. Do NOT use the time to work on another section.

Section 3

Math Test – No Calculator

25 MINUTES, 17 QUESTIONS

Turn to Section 3 of your answer sheet to answer the questions in this section.

DIRECTIONS

Questions **1-13** ask you to solve a problem, select the best answer among four choices, and fill in the corresponding circle on your answer sheet. Questions **14-17** ask you to solve a problem and enter your answer in a grid provided on your answer sheet. There are detailed instructions on entering answers into the grid before question 14. You may use your test booklet for scratch work.

NOTES

1. You **may not** use a calculator.
2. Variables and expressions represent real numbers unless stated otherwise.
3. Figures are drawn to scale unless stated otherwise.
4. Figures lie in a plane unless stated otherwise.
5. The domain of a function f is defined as the set of all real numbers x for which $f(x)$ is also a real number, unless stated otherwise.

REFERENCE

$A = \frac{1}{2}bh$

$a^2 + b^2 = c^2$

Special Triangles

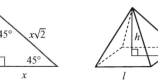

$V = \frac{1}{3}lwh$

$V = \frac{1}{3}\pi r^2 h$

$A = lw$

$V = lwh$

$V = \pi r^2 h$

$A = \pi r^2$

$C = 2\pi r$

$V = \frac{4}{3}\pi r^3$

There are 360° in a circle.

The sum of the angles in a triangle is 180°.

The number of radians of arc in a circle is 2π.

CONTINUE

1

If $xy + 2x = 5y + 5$, what is the value of x when $y = 3$?

A) 1

B) 4

C) 6

D) 8

2

If $2x + 6 = x + 12$, what is the value of x?

A) 1

B) 3

C) 6

D) 8

3

For which of the following functions is $f(-1) > f(1)$?

A) $f(x) = -4 + x$

B) $f(x) = 2x$

C) $f(x) = 7 - x$

D) $f(x) = -(3 - x)$

4

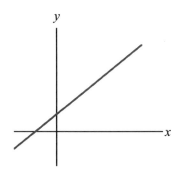

$f(x) = x + b$ is graphed above. Which of the following choices correctly represents the expression $f(-x) + 2$?

A)

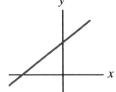

B)

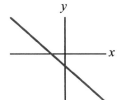

C)

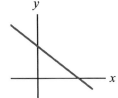

D)

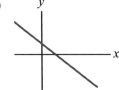

CONTINUE

5

If the sum of 3 consecutive even integers is greater than 20, what is the smallest possible value for the first integer?

A) 4

B) 6

C) 8

D) 10

6

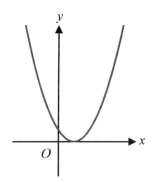

The figure above shows the graph of $y = (x-1)^2$. What is a possible value of x if $(x-1)^2 = 4$?

A) 2

B) 3

C) 4

D) 5

7

If $f(x) - f(x+1) = 2x - 5$ and $f(6) = 12$, what is the value of $f(5)$?

A) 5

B) 7

C) 17

D) 19

8

t	$d(t)$
0	1200
1	1260
2	1323
3	1389
4	1459

Joe has placed \$1200 into an investment account that pays 5% interest every year. The table above shows the amount of money in the account (rounded to the nearest dollar), $d(t)$, as a function of the number of years since Joe deposited the money, t. Which of the following equations best represents the relationship between t and $d(t)$?

A) $d(t) = 1200 + 1200(1.05t)$

B) $d(t) = 1200\left(\dfrac{t}{1.05}\right)$

C) $d(t) = 1200(1.05)^t$

D) $d(t) = 1200 + (0.05)(1200^t)$

CONTINUE

9

An enzyme takes 2 milliseconds to decompose a molecule of chemical A and 1 millisecond to decompose a molecule of chemical B. Molecules of chemicals A and B are mixed together, resulting in 12 molecules total. If the enzyme takes 16 milliseconds to decompose the mix of the two chemicals, which system of linear equations best represents this information?

A) $2x + y = 16$
   $x + y = 12$

B) $2x + y = 12$
   $x + y = 16$

C) $2x + y = 16$
   $x - y = 12$

D) $2x + y = 12$
   $x - y = 16$

10

Which of the following is a possible solution to the equation $x = x^{-2}$?

A) −1
B) 0
C) 1
D) 2

11

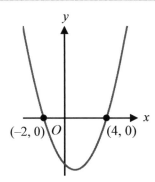

Of all the points (x, y) on the graph above, for what value of x is the value of y smallest?

A) 0
B) 1
C) 2
D) 3

CONTINUE

12

t	b
0	10
1	20
2	40
3	80
4	160

The table above shows the population of an invasive species of beetle that was introduced into a new habitat. Which of the following equations represents b, the population of the beetles, as a function of t, the number of years since the beetles were first introduced?

A) $b = 10(1 - t)^2$

B) $b = 10(t + 1)^2$

C) $b = 10(2^t)$

D) $b = 20(0.5)^{t + 1}$

13

x	y
0	9
1	16
2	25
3	36
4	49

The table above shows the values of y for certain values of x. Which of the following could represent the relationship between x and y?

A) $y = x^2 - x + 1$

B) $y = x^2 + 4x + 4$

C) $y = x^2 + 6x + 9$

D) $y = 4x^2 + 4x + 1$

CONTINUE

DIRECTIONS

Questions **14-17** ask you to solve a problem and enter your answer in the grid provided on your answer sheet. When completing grid-in questions:

1. You are required to bubble in the circles for your answers. It is recommended, but not required, that you also write your answer in the boxes above the columns of circles. Points will be awarded based only on whether the circles are filled in correctly.

2. Fill in only one circle in a column.

3. You can start your answer in any column as long as you can fit in the whole answer.

4. For questions 14-17, no answers will be negative numbers.

5. **Mixed Numbers,** such as $4\frac{2}{5}$, must be gridded as decimals or improper fractions, such as 4.4 or as 22/5. "42/5" will be read as "forty-two over five," not as "four and two-fifths."

6. If your answer is a **decimal** with more digits than will fit on the grid, you may round it or cut it off, but you must fill the entire grid.

7. If there are **multiple correct solutions** to a problem, all of them will be considered correct. Enter only **one** on the grid.

CONTINUE

14

$$4\sqrt{x} = 24$$

What is the value of x in the equation above?

15

If $3(x^{-3}) = \dfrac{1}{9}$, what is x^{-2}?

16

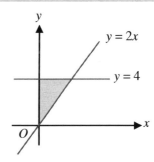

What is the area of the shaded region in the graph above?

17

10 years ago, Jane was twice as old as Mark is now. If in two years Jane will be three times as old as Mark is now, how old will Mark be in 4 years?

STOP

If you complete this section before the end of your allotted time, check your work on this section only. Do NOT use the time to work on another section.

Section 4

Math Test – Calculator

45 MINUTES, 31 QUESTIONS

Turn to Section 4 of your answer sheet to answer the questions in this section.

DIRECTIONS

Questions **1-27** ask you to solve a problem, select the best answer among four choices, and fill in the corresponding circle on your answer sheet. Questions **28-31** ask you to solve a problem and enter your answer in a grid provided on your answer sheet. There are detailed instructions on entering answers into the grid before question 28. You may use your test booklet for scratch work.

NOTES

1. You **may** use a calculator.
2. Variables and expressions represent real numbers unless stated otherwise.
3. Figures are drawn to scale unless stated otherwise.
4. Figures lie in a plane unless stated otherwise.
5. The domain of a function f is defined as the set of all real numbers x for which $f(x)$ is also a real number, unless stated otherwise.

REFERENCE

   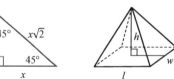

$A = \frac{1}{2}bh$ $a^2 + b^2 = c^2$ Special Triangles $V = \frac{1}{3}lwh$ $V = \frac{1}{3}\pi r^2 h$

$A = lw$ $V = lwh$ $V = \pi r^2 h$ $A = \pi r^2$ $V = \frac{4}{3}\pi r^3$

$C = 2\pi r$

There are 360° in a circle.

The sum of the angles in a triangle is 180°.

The number of radians of arc in a circle is 2π.

CONTINUE

1

$$x = 1$$

The value for x is defined above. What is the value of $(x - 1)(x + 4)$?

A) –4
B) –1
C) 0
D) 1

2

Which of the following expressions is equivalent to 2^{12}?

A) $2^7 \cdot 2^5$
B) $2^3 \cdot 2^4$
C) $(2^6)^6$
D) $2^6 + 2^6$

3

A study finds that a species of wren spends on average one hour in order to catch six insects. A female wren must catch 20 insects for herself and 8 insects for each of her chicks every day. If she has 5 chicks, how many hours per day does she have to spend catching insects to feed herself and her chicks?

A) 6
B) 8
C) 10
D) 12

4

For integers a and b, $a \mathbin{\#} b = a^2 - 2b$. If $a \mathbin{\#} 8 = 0$, which of the following statement(s) is (are) true?

I. $a \mathbin{\#} 8 = 8a$
II. $a \mathbin{\#} 8 = a^2 - 16$
III. $a = 4$
IV. $a = -4$

A) I only
B) II and III
C) II and IV
D) II, III and IV

5

$$\{2, 7, -2, 0, 8\}$$

A is a set of numbers shown above. If B is a set generated by halving each element in A, what is the range of B?

A) 10
B) 7
C) 5
D) 4

CONTINUE

6

A litigation firm is considering offering a special promotion to their clients. A lawyer normally charges a flat fee of $600 for 2 hours of consulting work. For each additional hour, he charges $400. If the firm offers a free bonus hour for an initial consultation, how much on average would the firm be charging, in dollars per hour, for 4 hours of consulting work?

A) 200
B) 250
C) 340
D) 400

7

If the sum of 50% of *m* and 50% of *n* is 75% of *m*, *n* is what percent of *m*?

A) 50%
B) 100%
C) 150%
D) 200%

8

A lab manager would like to spend 70% of the yearly budget on purchasing lab supplies. If he estimates that lab supplies will cost $140,000, how much money, in dollars, should he request for the year?

A) 98,000
B) 124,000
C) 150,000
D) 200,000

9

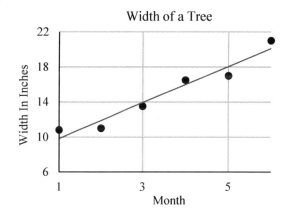

Width of a Tree

Forestry scientists have plotted a tree's growth over time, using its width as the primary measure. The graph above shows their results. According to the graph's trend line, how wide do the researchers predict that the tree will be at month 7?

A) Sixteen inches
B) Eighteen inches
C) Twenty inches
D) Twenty-two inches

CONTINUE

10

Music Download Packages

Single songs	$1.50 per song
10 songs	$13
Unlimited	$15 per month

The table above shows various packages offered by a music provider. If Samantha downloads 12 songs in one month, which of the following packages offers her the lowest price for that month?

A) Single songs
B) Ten songs and two single songs
C) Unlimited
D) Two packs of ten songs

11

The table below organizes a survey of 317 rocks found in different elevations into igneous, sedimentary, and metamorphic.

Survey of 317 Rocks

	Above 5,000 ft.	1,000-5,000 ft.	0-999 ft.	Total
Igneous	70	23	19	112
Sedimentary	5	20	35	60
Metamorphic	33	61	51	145
Total	108	104	105	317

Approximately what percent of sedimentary rocks were found below 1,000 ft.?

A) 58 percent
B) 33 percent
C) 11 percent
D) 8 percent

12

In a gorilla sanctuary in the Democratic Republic of the Congo, the median age of western lowland gorillas is 12 years, and the average age of Cross River gorillas is 12 years. Which of the following statements must be true?

A) The average age of both gorilla species is 12 years.
B) The median and the average age of Cross River gorillas are 12 years.
C) The average age of lowland gorillas is also equal to 12 years.
D) There is not enough information to compare the age of the two gorilla species.

CONTINUE

13

Two equations are modeled on a computer. Numbers in equation n increase according to the expression $n = 2^a$. Numbers in equation m increase according to the expression $m = 2 \times a + 8$. If a is the number of hours the model runs, how many hours does it take for n to equal m?

A) The number m will always be greater than the number n.

B) 1

C) 2

D) 4

14

When x is added to the group of numbers 24, 13, 60, 45, and 19, the group's range increases by 5. What is one possible value for x?

A) 65

B) 18

C) 0

D) –8

CONTINUE

Questions 15, 16, and 17 refer to the following information.

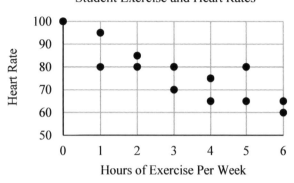

Student Exercise and Heart Rates

15

How many of the students surveyed exercise 3 or more hours per week?

A) Eight
B) Seven
C) Six
D) Five

16

What is the median heart rate of the students surveyed?

A) 75
B) 80
C) 85
D) 90

17

Based on the information, which of the following is true?

A) The average heart rate is equal to the median heart rate.
B) The average heart rate is less than the mode of the heart rate data.
C) The average heart rate is equal to the mode of the heart rate data.
D) The range of the heart rate data is greater than the mode of the heart rate data.

CONTINUE

18

An aquarium allocates a sum of money for the maintenance and feeding of its dolphins. Each dolphin tank costs $250 per day to staff and each tank can hold three dolphins. One dolphin eats $20 worth of food each day. If the aquarium has 12 dolphins, how much money must it budget per day to keep its dolphins?

A) $1,240
B) $1,400
C) $1,540
D) $1,600

20

If $x^2 + x = 20$, which of the following is a possible value for $x^2 - x$?

A) 10
B) 20
C) 30
D) 40

21

A company's total revenue is represented by the function $r = -x^2 + 17x$, where x is the average price of their product. Its production costs are represented by the function $c = 7x + 25$. What would be the company's average product price, in dollars, if they made no profit? (Profit is equal to $r - c$.)

A) 1
B) 5
C) 10
D) 25

19

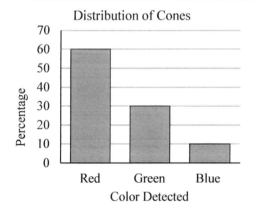

Distribution of Cones

Cones are cells on the retina of the eye that allow us to see color. Cones can detect one of three colors—red, green, or blue. The graphic above shows the percentage of the total number of cones that can detect each color. If a sample of retina tissue has 200 cones, how many cones would we expect to detect the color red?

A) 20
B) 30
C) 60
D) 120

CONTINUE

22

The median of a group of positive integers is m. The group's average is a, and the range is r. Which of the following statements is always true?

A) If $m > a$, then more numbers are greater than the median than are smaller than the median.

B) If $m < a$, then more numbers are smaller than the median than are greater than the median.

C) If a is equal to half of the sum of the smallest and largest number, then r is equal to twice the difference of a and the smallest number.

D) If $a = r$, then half of the integers are larger than a and half of the numbers are smaller than a.

23

x	$f(x)$
1	1
3	5

The table above gives values for the linear function $f(x)$. What is the value of $f(-4)$?

A) -9

B) -8

C) -7

D) 7

24

$$y - 3 = 2x + 10$$
$$2x + 3y = -1$$

If the two equations above intersect at the point (p, q), what is the value of pq?

A) -15

B) -5

C) 0

D) 3

25

In the time it takes Computer A to make 100 calculations, Computer B can make 140 calculations. If it takes Computer A 25 seconds to make 375 calculations, how many minutes does it take for Computer B to make 6,300 calculations?

A) 7

B) 6

C) 5

D) 4

CONTINUE

26

$$y = 2x^2$$
$$y^2 = x^2 + 6x + 9$$

What is a possible solution for x in the system of equations above?

A) -3

B) -1

C) 2

D) 3

27

2, 5, 8, 9, 11

The number a is added to the set of numbers listed above. If a is an integer and $0 < a < 10$, which of the following could be the new average of the set of numbers?

    I. 5

   II. 7

  III. 8

A) I only

B) II only

C) I and II only

D) II and III only

CONTINUE

DIRECTIONS

Questions **28-31** ask you to solve a problem and enter your answer in the grid provided on your answer sheet. When completing grid-in questions:

1. You are required to bubble in the circles for your answers. It is recommended, but not required, that you also write your answer in the boxes above the columns of circles. Points will be awarded based only on whether the circles are filled in correctly.

2. Fill in only one circle in a column.

3. You can start your answer in any column as long as you can fit in the whole answer.

4. For questions 28-31, no answers will be negative numbers.

5. **Mixed Numbers,** such as $4\frac{2}{5}$, must be gridded as decimals or improper fractions, such as 4.4 or as 22/5. "42/5" will be read as "forty-two over five," not as "four and two-fifths."

6. If your answer is a **decimal** with more digits than will fit on the grid, you may round it or cut it off, but you must fill the entire grid.

7. If there are **multiple correct solutions** to a problem, all of them will be considered correct. Enter only **one** on the grid.

CONTINUE

28

If a number half as big as *x* is subtracted from a number 3 times as big as *x*, the resulting value is what percent of *x*?

29

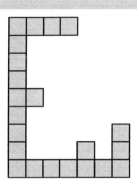

22 identical squares have been arranged as in the figure above. If the area of the shaded region is 198, what is the perimeter of the figure?

CONTINUE

Questions 30, and 31 refer to the following information.

The graph below shows gasoline prices, in dollars per gallon, for four states. The cost of transportation in each state is determined by that state's gasoline price and the number of miles of transportation required. After analysis, it is estimated that the average semi-truck used in commercial transportation uses one gallon of gasoline for every 7 miles of travel.

Gasoline Prices by State

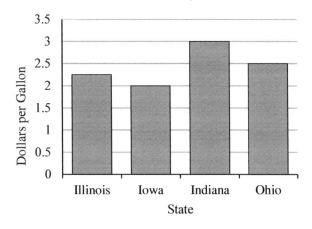

30

One semi-truck is travelling in Iowa, purchasing gasoline in Iowa. Another semi-truck is travelling in Ohio, purchasing gasoline in Ohio. If both trucks purchase 100 dollars of gasoline, how many more miles can the Iowa truck travel than the Ohio truck?

31

A semi-truck transports 150 crates of supplies from Iowa to Ohio. The truck driver purchases 20 gallons of gas in Iowa and travels until he runs out of fuel. He then buys another 50 gallons of gas in Illinois and travels until he runs out of fuel. Finally, he buys 10 gallons of gas in Indiana and completes the trip to Ohio. If he uses all of his gas to arrive at his destination, how much should he charge for his supplies, in dollars per crate, in order to break even? (Round your answer to the nearest cent.)

STOP

If you complete this section before the end of your allotted time, check your work on this section only. Do NOT use the time to work on another section.

Chapter 3
Answers and Scoring

SECTION 1
ANSWERS

Practice Test 1 Answers
Part 1

Section 1

1. C	13. B	25. B	37. C
2. A	14. C	26. A	38. A
3. B	15. C	27. B	39. D
4. C	16. D	28. C	40. B
5. B	17. A	29. B	41. C
6. A	18. A	30. B	42. B
7. B	19. B	31. C	43. A
8. D	20. B	32. C	44. B
9. C	21. C	33. A	45. D
10. D	22. A	34. A	46. A
11. C	23. A	35. B	47. A
12. B	24. B	36. B	

Section 2

1. B	12. B	23. A	34. C
2. C	13. A	24. D	35. D
3. C	14. C	25. B	36. C
4. C	15. C	26. B	37. D
5. B	16. C	27. D	38. C
6. B	17. B	28. C	39. A
7. B	18. C	29. C	40. B
8. C	19. C	30. A	41. C
9. D	20. A	31. A	42. C
10. A	21. C	32. B	43. D
11. B	22. A	33. C	44. C

Section 3

1. C	6. D	11. B	16. 1
2. B	7. D	12. B	17. 3
3. D	8. C	13. B	
4. A	9. C	14. 12	
5. C	10. C	15. 4	

Section 4

1. C	9. C	17. C	25. C
2. C	10. A	18. C	26. C
3. B	11. D	19. C	27. D
4. C	12. B	20. C	28. 65
5. D	13. D	21. D	29. 5
6. B	14. C	22. C	30. 3.4
7. B	15. C	23. A	31. 11.8
8. B	16. A	24. C	

PRACTICE TEST 3 ANSWERS
PART 3

SECTION 1

1. C	13. A	25. C	37. B
2. C	14. D	26. B	38. A
3. D	15. B	27. C	39. B
4. A	16. C	28. B	40. C
5. C	17. B	29. B	41. B
6. B	18. A	30. A	42. B
7. A	19. C	31. D	43. B
8. C	20. C	32. B	44. C
9. C	21. B	33. B	45. B
10. C	22. C	34. A	46. A
11. B	23. A	35. B	47. D
12. A	24. D	36. B	

SECTION 2

1. D	12. D	23. C	34. D
2. B	13. B	24. A	35. D
3. D	14. B	25. C	36. C
4. B	15. A	26. C	37. C
5. C	16. C	27. D	38. C
6. C	17. D	28. B	39. B
7. B	18. C	29. D	40. A
8. C	19. C	30. D	41. C
9. D	20. B	31. C	42. D
10. A	21. D	32. A	43. C
11. D	22. B	33. B	44. B

SECTION 3

1. B	6. B	11. B	16. 4
2. C	7. C	12. C	17. 16
3. C	8. C	13. C	
4. C	9. A	14. 36	
5. B	10. C	15. $\frac{1}{9}$	

SECTION 4

1. C	9. D	17. B	25. C
2. A	10. C	18. A	26. B
3. C	11. A	19. D	27. B
4. D	12. D	20. C	28. 250
5. C	13. D	21. B	29. 138
6. B	14. A	22. C	30. 70
7. A	15. A	23. A	31. 1.22
8. D	16. B	24. A	

SECTION 2
SCORING

THE SCORING SYSTEM
PART 1

The new PSAT will have three **test scores** on a scale from 8 to 38. There will be one test score for each test: the Reading Test, the Writing Test, and the Math Test. The Reading Test score and the Writing and Language Test score will be added together and converted to a single **section score** in Evidence-Based Reading and Writing; there will also be a section score in Math based on the Math Test Score. The section scores will be on a scale from 160 to 760. Added together, they will form the **composite score** for the whole test, on a scale from 320 to 1520.

PSAT Scoring	
Test Scores (8 to 38)	• Reading Test • Writing Test • Math Test
Section Scores (160 to 760)	• Evidence-Based Reading and Writing • Math
Composite Score (320 to 1520)	• Math (Section Score) + Evidence-Based Reading and Writing (Section Score)

SUBSCORES

The College Board will also be reporting new types of PSAT scores. There will be seven **subscores** based on particular question types within each test section. Some subscores will be based on question types found in the Reading and Writing Tests, while others will relate only to questions found on the Math Test. Subscores will be reported on a scale from 1 to 15.

Seven subscores will be reported: Heart of Algebra, Problem Solving and Data Analysis, Passport to Advanced Math, Expression of Ideas, Standard English Conventions, Words in Context, and Command of Evidence. Each score will be based on a range of 14 to 24 questions that test the particular skill named.

Find scoring sheets with detailed scoring information at:
ivyglobal.com/study

Scoring your Tests

PART 2

To score your tests, first use the answer key to mark each of your responses right or wrong. Then, calculate your **raw score** for each section by counting up the number of correct responses. Use the tables below to help you calculate your scores:

Practice Test 1 – Raw Score

Section	# of Questions Correct
1. Reading	_____
2. Writing	_____
3. Math: No-Calculator	_____
4. Math: Calculator	_____

Raw Score for Reading (Section 1): _____

Raw Score for Writing (Section 2): _____

Raw Score for Math (Section 3 + 4): _____

Practice Test 2 – Raw Score

Section	# of Questions Correct
1. Reading	_____
2. Writing	_____
3. Math: No-Calculator	_____
4. Math: Calculator	_____

Raw Score for Reading (Section 1): _____

Raw Score for Writing (Section 2): _____

Raw Score for Math (Section 3 + 4): _____

Practice Test 3 – Raw Score

Section	# of Questions Correct
1. Reading	_____
2. Writing	_____
3. Math: No-Calculator	_____
4. Math: Calculator	_____

Raw Score for Reading (Section 1): _____

Raw Score for Writing (Section 2): _____

Raw Score for Math (Section 3 + 4): _____

SCALED SCORES

Once you have found your raw score for each section, convert it into an approximate **scaled test score** using the following charts. To find a scaled test score for each section, find the row in the Raw Score column that corresponds to your raw score for that section, and then check the column for the section you are scoring in the same row. For example, if you had a raw score of 39 for reading, then your scaled reading test score would be 33. Keep in mind that these scaled scores are estimates only. Your actual SAT score will be scaled against the scores of all other high school students taking the test on your test date.

Raw Score	Math Scaled Score	Reading Scaled Score	Writing Scaled Score	Raw Score	Math Scaled Score	Reading Scaled Score	Writing Scaled Score
48	38			23	24	22	21
47	38	38		22	23	21	20
46	37	38		21	22	20	20
45	37	37		20	21	19	19
44	36	36	38	19	20	18	18
43	35	35	38	18	19	18	17
42	35	35	37	17	18	17	16
41	34	34	36	16	17	15	15
40	34	34	35	15	16	14	14
39	33	33	34	14	15	13	13
38	33	33	33	13	14	12	12
37	32	32	32	12	13	11	11
36	32	32	31	11	12	10	10
35	31	31	30	10	11	9	10
34	31	30	29	9	10	8	9
33	31	30	28	8	9	8	9
32	30	29	27	7	8	8	8
31	30	29	26	6	8	8	8
30	29	28	25	5	8	8	8
29	29	27	24	4	8	8	8
28	28	27	23	3	8	8	8
27	27	26	23	2	8	8	8
26	27	25	22	1	8	8	8
25	26	24	22	0	8	8	8
24	25	23	21				

Use the table below to record your scaled scores:

Practice Test 1 – Scaled Scores

Scaled Score for Reading (Out of 38):   _____

Scaled Score for Writing (Out of 38):   _____

Scaled Score for Math (Out of 38):   _____

Practice Test 2 – Scaled Scores

Scaled Score for Reading (Out of 38):   _____

Scaled Score for Writing (Out of 38):   _____

Scaled Score for Math (Out of 38):   _____

Practice Test 3 – Scaled Scores

Scaled Score for Reading (Out of 38):   _____

Scaled Score for Writing (Out of 38):   _____

Scaled Score for Math (Out of 38):   _____

Find detailed scoring information (including subscores and cross-test scores) at:

ivyglobal.com/study

SECTION SCORE CONVERSION

You can look up your section score out of 760 below. To find your overall score, combine your section score for Reading + Writing with your section score for Math to get your total score out of 1520.

READING + WRITING

Scaled Score	Section Score	Scaled Score	Section Score	Scaled Score	Section Score
76	720-760	55	510-590	35	310-390
75	710-760	54	500-580	34	300-380
74	700-760	53	490-570	33	290-370
73	690-760	52	480-560	32	280-360
72	680-760	51	470-550	31	270-350
71	670-750	50	460-540	30	260-340
70	660-740	49	450-530	29	250-330
69	650-730	48	440-520	28	240-320
68	640-720	47	430-510	27	230-310
67	630-710	46	420-500	26	220-300
66	620-700	45	410-490	25	210-290
65	610-690	44	400-480	24	200-280
64	600-680	43	390-470	23	190-270
63	590-670	42	380-460	22	180-260
62	580-660	41	370-450	21	170-250
61	570-650	40	360-440	20	160-240
60	560-640	39	350-430	19	160-230
59	550-630	38	340-420	18	160-220
58	540-620	37	330-410	17	160-210
57	530-610	36	320-400	16	160-200
56	520-600				

MATH

Total Points	Section Score	Total Points	Section Score
38	720-760	22	400-480
37	700-760	21	380-460
36	680-760	20	360-440
35	660-740	19	340-420
34	640-720	18	320-400
33	620-700	17	300-380
32	600-680	16	280-360
31	580-660	15	260-340
30	560-640	14	240-320
29	540-620	13	220-300
28	520-600	12	200-280
27	500-580	11	180-260
26	480-560	10	160-240
25	460-540	9	160-220
24	440-520	8	160-200
23	420-500		

Use the tables below to record your section scores and to calculate your overall scores:

Practice Test 1

Reading + Writing Section Score		Math Section Score		Overall Score (320-1520)
_____	+	_____	=	_____

Practice Test 2

Reading + Writing Section Score		Math Section Score		Overall Score (320-1520)
_____	+	_____	=	_____

Practice Test 3

Reading + Writing Section Score		Math Section Score		Overall Score (320-1520)
_____	+	_____	=	_____

50th ANNIVERSARY

DUNKIRK

1940~1990